Windows™ 3.1

VISUAL  SERIES

by: maranGraphics' Development Group

Corporate Sales	Canadian Trade Sales
Contact maranGraphics	Contact Prentice Hall Canada
Phone: (905) 890-3300, ext.206	Phone: (416) 293-3621
(800) 469-6616, ext.206	(800) 567-3800
Fax: (905) 890-9434	Fax: (416) 299-2529

Windows™ 3.1 Visual 3-D Series

Trademark Acknowledgments

©1993
maranGraphics, Inc.

The animated characters are the copyright of maranGraphics, Inc.

Acknowledgments

Thanks to John Hodgins, Elliot Katz and Allan Watson of Microsoft Canada Inc. for their support and consultation.

Special thanks to Wendi B. Ewbank for her patience, insight and humor throughout the project.

Thanks to the dedicated staff of maranGraphics, including Robin Clark, David de Haas, Brad Hilderley, Paul Lofthouse, Judy Maran, Maxine Maran, Robert Maran, Sherry Maran, Suzanna Pereira, Tamara Poliquin, Dave Ross, Christie Van Duin, Carol Walthers and Kelleigh Wing.

Finally, to Richard Maran who originated the easy-to-use graphic format of this guide. Thank you for your inspiration and guidance.

Credits

Author & Architect: Ruth Maran	*Screens and Layout:* Béla Korcsog
Consultant: Wendi Blouin Ewbank	*Technical Consultant:* Eric Feistmantl
Layout: Jim C. Leung	*Editor:* Judy Maran
Illustrator: Dave Ross	*Proofreader:* David Hendricks

Table of Contents

Introduction
to
Windows

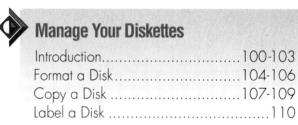

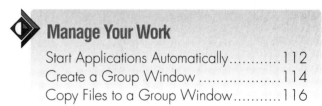

Working with Windows

Print

Control Panel

Run DOS in Windows

Sharing Data

Improve Windows Performance

Windows enables you to:

◆ Run one or more applications at the same time.

◆ Share information between applications.

◆ Manage your files.

◆ Work with peripheral devices such as your printer.

Note: The terms program and application are used interchangeably.

| Getting Started | Windows Basics | Help | Manage Your Applications | Manage Your Directories | Manage Your Files | Manage Your Diskettes | Manage Your Work |

Introduction
Start Windows
Mouse Basics
Using the Menus
Exit Windows

Windows enforces basic rules that all applications must follow.

Applications perform tasks such as word processing and spreadsheet analysis. Windows controls how these applications input and output their data.

Windows controls how an application interacts with you.

Windows provides tools to store and organize the files on your computer.

START
WINDOWS

Windows offers an easy, graphical approach to using your computer.

`C:\> WIN_`

1 To start Microsoft® Windows™ 3.1 from MS-DOS, type **WIN** and then press `Enter`.

Let's Assume...

◆ Windows 3.1 is installed on your hard drive in a directory named WINDOWS.

◆ You use a mouse with Windows 3.1.

INTRODUCTION TO WINDOWS

| Getting Started | Windows Basics | Help | Manage Your Applications | Manage Your Directories | Manage Your Files | Manage Your Diskettes | Manage Your Work |

◆ Each time you start Windows, the **Program Manager** window appears. A window is a rectangle on your screen that contains icons or displays a document.

*Note: An **icon** is a graphic that represents an application, a document or any other element.*

The Program Manager window contains two types of icons:

◆ A **program-item icon** represents a program that you can start from Windows (example: **File Manager**).

◆ A **group icon** organizes programs into groups (example: **Games**). A group icon can contain up to 50 program-item icons.

Your computer screen is called a desktop. You can open and display multiple windows on your desktop.

MOUSE BASICS

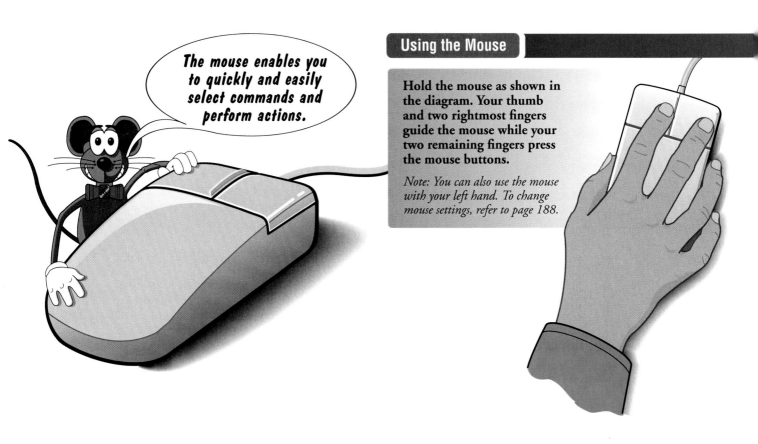

The mouse enables you to quickly and easily select commands and perform actions.

Using the Mouse

Hold the mouse as shown in the diagram. Your thumb and two rightmost fingers guide the mouse while your two remaining fingers press the mouse buttons.

Note: You can also use the mouse with your left hand. To change mouse settings, refer to page 188.

Moving the Mouse Pointer

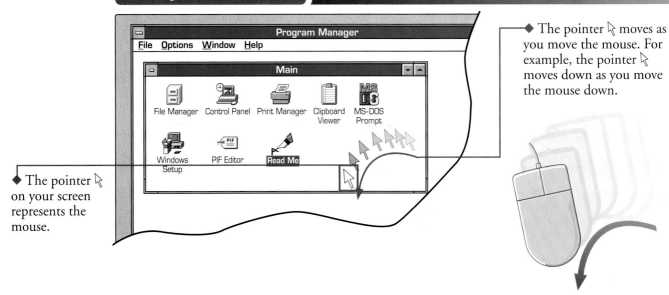

◆ The pointer on your screen represents the mouse.

◆ The pointer moves as you move the mouse. For example, the pointer moves down as you move the mouse down.

| Getting Started | Windows Basics | Help | Manage Your Applications | Manage Your Directories | Manage Your Files | Manage Your Diskettes | Manage Your Work |

Introduction
Start Windows
Mouse Basics
Using the Menus
Exit Windows

◆ The mouse has a left and right button. You can use these buttons to:

➡️ start programs

➡️ select commands

➡️ choose options

➡️ move icons

Note: You will use the left button most of the time.

◆ Under the mouse is a ball that senses movement. To ensure smooth motion of the mouse, occasionally remove and clean this ball.

Mouse Terms

TERM	WHAT IT MEANS
Point	Move the mouse until the pointer ▷ on your screen is over the desired object.
Click	Quickly press and release the left mouse button.
Double-click	Quickly press and release the left mouse button twice.
Drag	When the pointer ▷ is over an object, press and hold down the left mouse button and then move the mouse.

USING THE MENUS

You can open a menu to display a list of related commands. You can then select a command to accomplish a task.

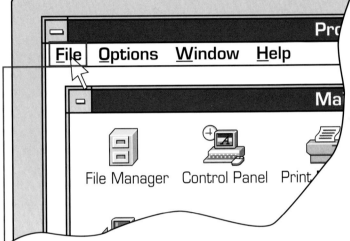

1 To open a menu, move the mouse ⊳ over the menu name (example: **File**) and then press the left button.

USING THE KEYBOARD

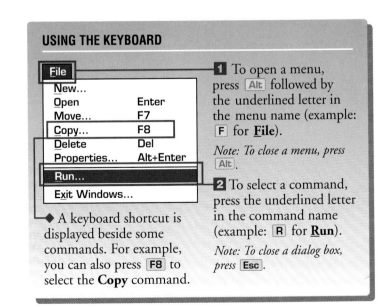

1 To open a menu, press `Alt` followed by the underlined letter in the menu name (example: `F` for **File**).

Note: To close a menu, press `Alt`.

2 To select a command, press the underlined letter in the command name (example: `R` for **Run**).

Note: To close a dialog box, press `Esc`.

◆ A keyboard shortcut is displayed beside some commands. For example, you can also press `F8` to select the **Copy** command.

INTRODUCTION TO WINDOWS

| Getting Started | Windows Basics | Help | Manage Your Applications | Manage Your Directories | Manage Your Files | Manage Your Diskettes | Manage Your Work |

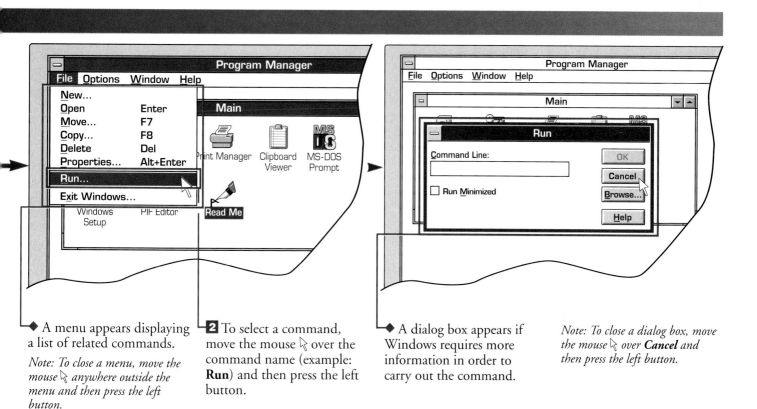

◆ A menu appears displaying a list of related commands.

Note: To close a menu, move the mouse ⟲ anywhere outside the menu and then press the left button.

2 To select a command, move the mouse ⟲ over the command name (example: **Run**) and then press the left button.

◆ A dialog box appears if Windows requires more information in order to carry out the command.

*Note: To close a dialog box, move the mouse ⟲ over **Cancel** and then press the left button.*

KEY COMBINATIONS

>Click<   >Click<   >Click<   >Click<

◆ If key names are separated by a plus sign (**+**), press and hold down the first key before pressing the second key (example: `Alt` + `Enter`).

◆ If key names are separated by a comma (**,**), press and release the first key before pressing the second key (example: `Alt` , `H`).

DIMMED COMMANDS

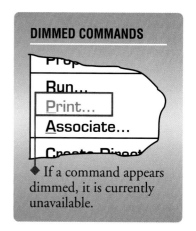

◆ If a command appears dimmed, it is currently unavailable.

Exiting Windows will return you to MS-DOS. You must always exit Windows before turning off your computer. Failure to do so may damage files stored on your hard drive.

Exit Windows

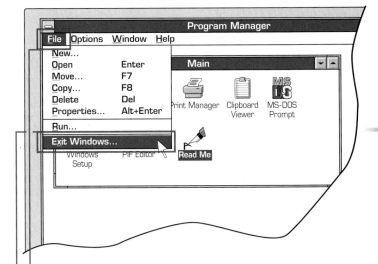

1 Move the mouse ⬚ over **File** and then press the left button.

2 Move the mouse ⬚ over **Exit Windows** and then press the left button.

Press Alt + F4

SAVE SETTINGS ON EXIT

Options
Auto Arrange
Minimize on Use
√ Save Settings on Exit

Your screen displays an arrangement of group windows and icons. You can save this arrangement so your screen appears the same way the next time you start Windows.

1 Move the mouse ⬚ over **Options** and then press the left button.

◆ A check mark (✓) displayed beside **Save Settings on Exit** indicates the command is **on**.

2 To leave the command on, press Alt to close the **Options** menu.

Note: To turn the command **off**, *move the mouse* ⬚ *over* **Save Settings on Exit** *and then press the left button.*

INTRODUCTION   TO   WINDOWS

| Getting Started | Windows Basics | Help | Manage Your Applications | Manage Your Directories | Manage Your Files | Manage Your Diskettes | Manage Your Work |

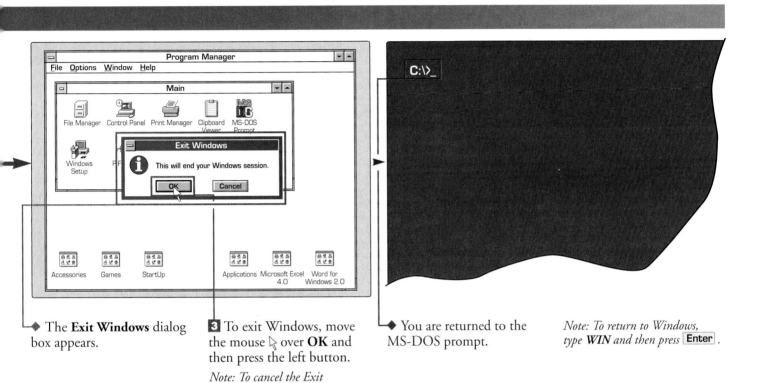

◆ The **Exit Windows** dialog box appears.

3 To exit Windows, move the mouse ⃕ over **OK** and then press the left button.

*Note: To cancel the Exit command, move the mouse ⃕ over **Cancel** and then press the left button.*

◆ You are returned to the MS-DOS prompt.

*Note: To return to Windows, type **WIN** and then press* Enter .

MOVE
A WINDOW

You can move a window from one location to another. This enables you to organize your desktop and display windows previously hidden from view.

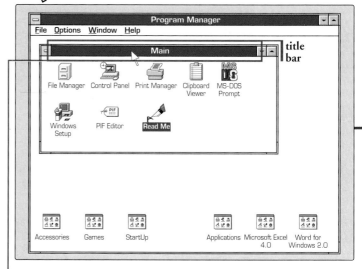

1 To move a window (example: **Main**), move the mouse ⬚ over its title bar and then press and hold down the left button.

Getting Started	Windows Basics	Help	Manage Your Applications	Manage Your Directories	Manage Your Files	Manage Your Diskettes	Manage Your Work

Move a Window
Size a Window
Move and Arrange Icons
Auto Arrange Icons
Minimize a Window
Restore an Icon

Maximize a Window
Restore a Window
Open Group Windows
Switch Between Group Windows
Cascade and Tile Group Windows
Scroll Through a Window

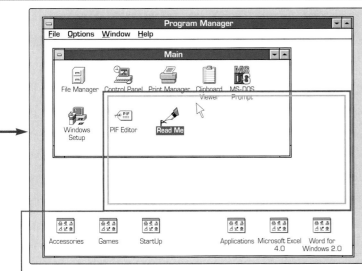

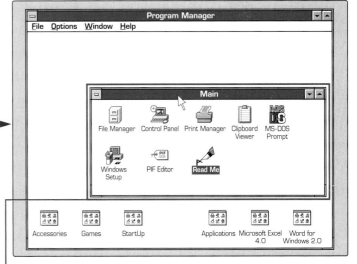

2 Still holding down the button, drag the window to a new location.

◆ A gray rectangle indicates the new location.

*Note: You cannot move a group window outside the **Program Manager** window.*

3 Release the button and the window jumps to the new position.

Note: To cancel the move, press Esc *before releasing the button in step* **3**.

SIZE
A WINDOW

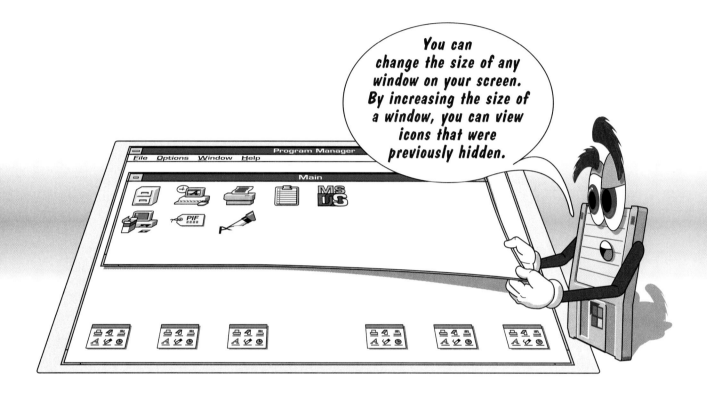

You can change the size of any window on your screen. By increasing the size of a window, you can view icons that were previously hidden.

Size a Window

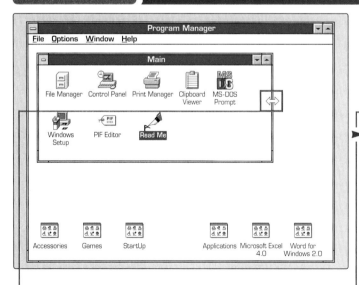

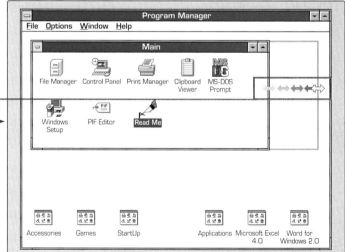

1 To change the size of a window, move the mouse ⟨ over the right or left edge of the window (⟨ becomes ⟷).

2 Press and hold down the left button as you drag the edge of the window to the desired size.

◆ A gray outline indicates the new size.

Getting Started	**Windows Basics**	Help	Manage Your Applications	Manage Your Directories	Manage Your Files	Manage Your Diskettes	Manage Your Work

Move a Window
Size a Window
Move and Arrange Icons
Auto Arrange Icons
Minimize a Window
Restore an Icon

Maximize a Window
Restore a Window
Open Group Windows
Switch Between Group Windows
Cascade and Tile Group Windows
Scroll Through a Window

You can use the method described below to size a window vertically.

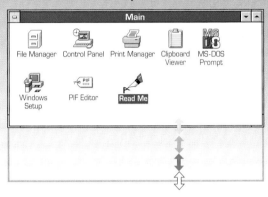

You can use the method described below to size a window horizontally and vertically at the same time.

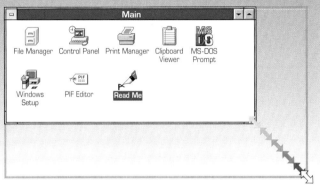

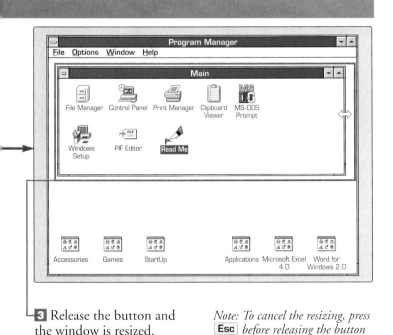

TIPS

◆ You can increase or decrease the size of a window from any edge or corner.

◆ When you size a window, some icons may become hidden. To view them, refer to "Scroll Through a Window" on page 28.

3 Release the button and the window is resized.

Note: To cancel the resizing, press **Esc** *before releasing the button in step* **3**.

MOVE AND ARRANGE ICONS

You can move an icon to a more suitable location in a window or have Windows automatically arrange the icons for you.

Move an Icon

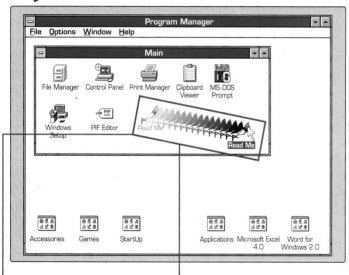

1 Move the mouse ▷ over the icon you want to move (example: **Read Me**).

2 Press and hold down the left button as you drag the icon to a new position in the window.

3 Release the button and the icon stays in the new position.

*Note: You cannot move an icon if the **Auto Arrange** command is **on**. For more information, refer to page 18.*

Getting Started	Windows Basics	Help	Manage Your Applications	Manage Your Directories	Manage Your Files	Manage Your Diskettes	Manage Your Work

Move a Window
Size a Window
Move and Arrange Icons
Auto Arrange Icons
Minimize a Window
Restore an Icon

Maximize a Window
Restore a Window
Open Group Windows
Switch Between Group Windows
Cascade and Tile Group Windows
Scroll Through a Window

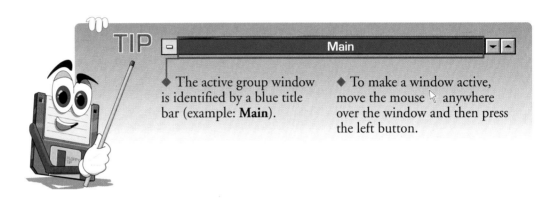

TIP

◆ The active group window is identified by a blue title bar (example: **Main**).

◆ To make a window active, move the mouse ⍽ anywhere over the window and then press the left button.

Arrange Icons

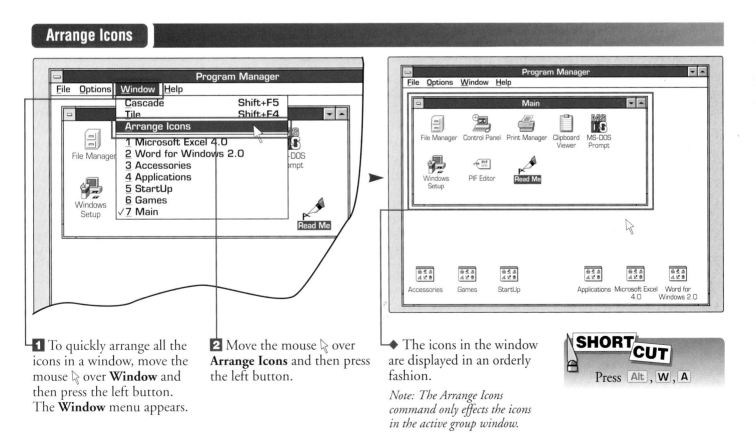

1 To quickly arrange all the icons in a window, move the mouse ⍽ over **Window** and then press the left button. The **Window** menu appears.

2 Move the mouse ⍽ over **Arrange Icons** and then press the left button.

◆ The icons in the window are displayed in an orderly fashion.

Note: The Arrange Icons command only effects the icons in the active group window.

SHORT**CUT**
Press Alt , W , A

AUTO ARRANGE ICONS

If you change the size of a window and the Auto Arrange command is on, Windows will automatically rearrange the icons in that window for you.

Auto Arrange Icons

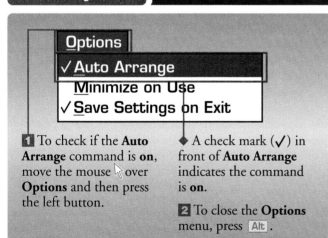

1 To check if the **Auto Arrange** command is **on**, move the mouse over **Options** and then press the left button.

◆ A check mark (✓) in front of **Auto Arrange** indicates the command is **on**.

2 To close the **Options** menu, press Alt.

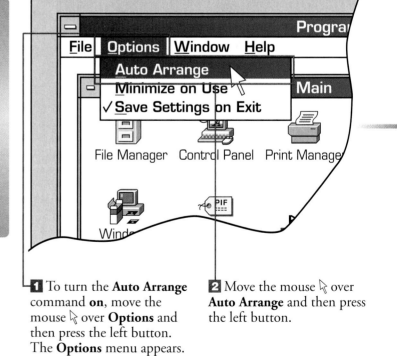

1 To turn the **Auto Arrange** command **on**, move the mouse over **Options** and then press the left button. The **Options** menu appears.

2 Move the mouse over **Auto Arrange** and then press the left button.

| Getting Started | **Windows Basics** | Help | Manage Your Applications | Manage Your Directories | Manage Your Files | Manage Your Diskettes | Manage Your Work |

Move a Window
Size a Window
Move and Arrange Icons
Auto Arrange Icons
Minimize a Window
Restore an Icon

Maximize a Window
Restore a Window
Open Group Windows
Switch Between Group Windows
Cascade and Tile Group Windows
Scroll Through a Window

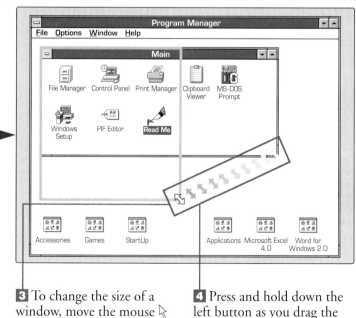

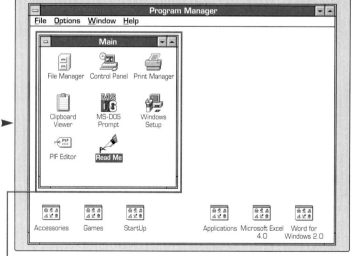

3 To change the size of a window, move the mouse ⟲ over any edge or corner of the window and ⟲ changes to ⤡.

4 Press and hold down the left button as you drag the window to the desired size.

5 Release the button and the window is resized.

◆ The icons automatically rearrange to fit neatly within the window.

MINIMIZE A WINDOW

RESTORE AN ICON

When you finish working with a window, you can minimize (reduce) it to an icon. This provides you with more working space on your screen.

▼ Minimize a Window

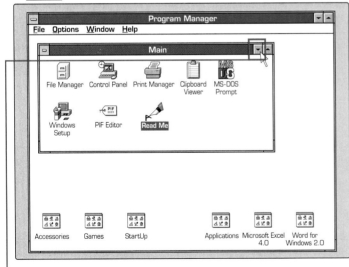

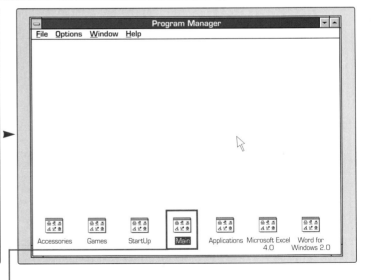

1 To reduce a window to an icon, move the mouse ⬚ over its **Minimize** button and then press the left button.

◆ The window is reduced to an icon.

Getting Started	Windows Basics	Help	Manage Your Applications	Manage Your Directories	Manage Your Files	Manage Your Diskettes	Manage Your Work

Move a Window
Size a Window
Move and Arrange Icons
Auto Arrange Icons
Minimize a Window
Restore an Icon

Maximize a Window
Restore a Window
Open Group Windows
Switch Between Group Windows
Cascade and Tile Group Windows
Scroll Through a Window

You can restore an icon to a window to display its contents. The window returns to its original size.

Restore an Icon

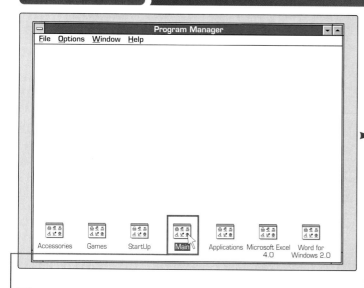

1 To restore an icon to a window, move the mouse over the icon (example: **Main**) and then quickly press the left button twice.

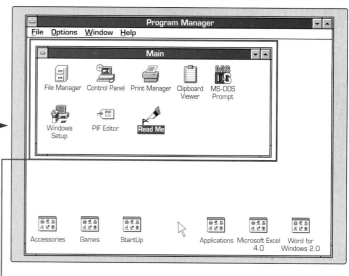

◆ The icon is restored to a window.

Maximize a Window

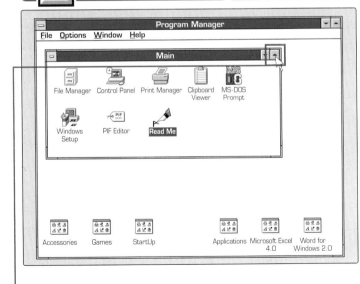

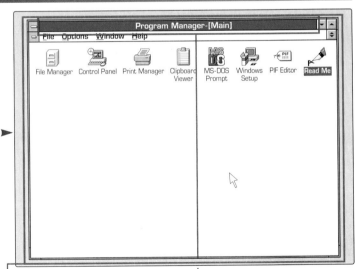

1 To enlarge a window (example: **Main**), move the mouse ⌖ over its **Maximize** button and then press the left button.

◆ The window enlarges to fill the entire area in the **Program Manager** window.

◆ The title bar is now shared. The name of the group window appears in square brackets (example: [**Main**]).

Getting Started	**Windows Basics**	Help	Manage Your Applications	Manage Your Directories	Manage Your Files	Manage Your Diskettes	Manage Your Work

Move a Window	**Maximize a Window**
Size a Window	**Restore a Window**
Move and Arrange Icons	Open Group Windows
Auto Arrange Icons	Switch Between Group Windows
Minimize a Window	Cascade and Tile Group Windows
Restore an Icon	Scroll Through a Window

You can restore a window to its original size.

Restore a Window

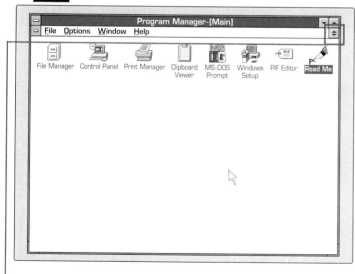

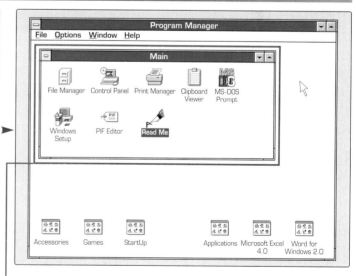

1 To restore a window (example: **Main**), move the mouse over its **Restore** button and then press the left button.

◆ The window is restored to its original size.

You can have several windows open at the same time. However, you can only work with the active window. To work with another window, you must first switch to it.

Open Group Windows

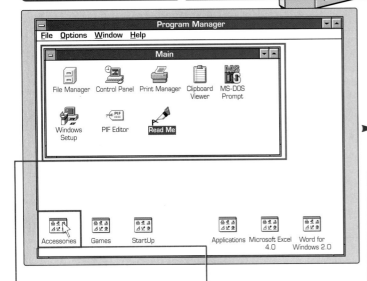

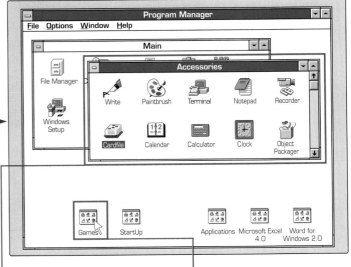

◆ The first time you start Windows, the **Main** group window is open.

1 To open another group window (example: **Accessories**), move the mouse ⧀ over its icon and then quickly press the left button twice.

◆ The window opens and becomes the active window.

◆ You can only work with the active window which displays a blue title bar.

2 To open another group window (example: **Games**), move the mouse ⧀ over its icon and then quickly press the left button twice.

Getting Started	**Windows Basics**	Help	Manage Your Applications	Manage Your Directories	Manage Your Files	Manage Your Diskettes	Manage Your Work

Move a Window
Size a Window
Move and Arrange Icons
Auto Arrange Icons
Minimize a Window
Restore an Icon

Maximize a Window
Restore a Window
Open Group Windows
Switch Between Group Windows
Cascade and Tile Group Windows
Scroll Through a Window

TIP

Think of each window as a separate piece of paper. When you open a window, you are placing a new piece of paper on your screen. Sometimes, the pieces of paper overlap.

Switch Between Group Windows

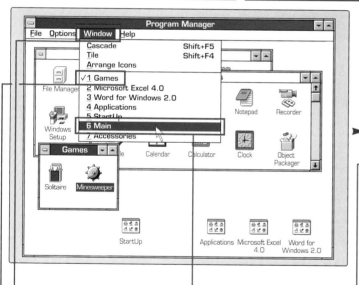

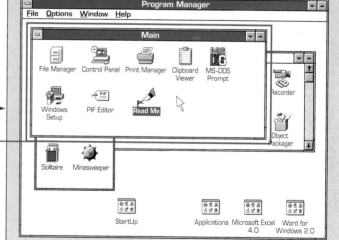

1 To switch to another group window, move the mouse ▷ over **Window** and then press the left button. The **Window** menu appears.

◆ A check mark (✓) is displayed beside the name of the active group window (example: **Games**).

2 Move the mouse ▷ over the name of the window you want to switch to (example: **Main**) and then press the left button.

◆ The window you selected now becomes the active window (example: **Main**).

Note: This method is useful if the group window you want to view is completely covered by another window.

SHORT CUT

Move the mouse ▷ over the window you want to switch to and then press the left button.

CASCADE AND TILE GROUP WINDOWS

If you have several group windows open, some of them may be hidden from view. The Cascade command allows you to display all your open group windows by overlapping them.

Cascade Group Windows

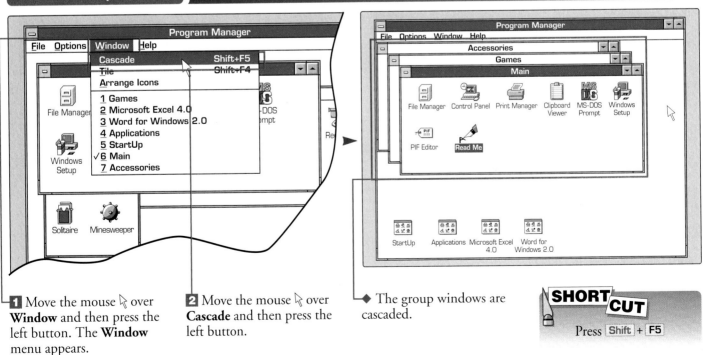

1 Move the mouse ⌖ over **Window** and then press the left button. The **Window** menu appears.

2 Move the mouse ⌖ over **Cascade** and then press the left button.

◆ The group windows are cascaded.

SHORT CUT

Press **Shift** + **F5**

Getting Started	Windows Basics	Help	Manage Your Applications	Manage Your Directories	Manage Your Files	Manage Your Diskettes	Manage Your Work

Move a Window   Maximize a Window
Size a Window   Restore a Window
Move and Arrange Icons   Open Group Windows
Auto Arrange Icons   Switch Between Group Windows
Minimize a Window   **Cascade and Tile Group Windows**
Restore an Icon   Scroll Through a Window

The Tile command lets you display all your open group windows side-by-side without overlapping them. This enables you to view the contents of each window.

Tile Group Windows

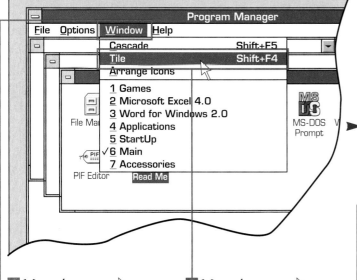

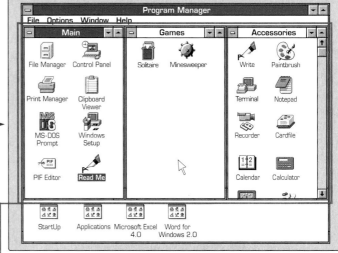

1 Move the mouse ⌖ over **Window** and then press the left button. The **Window** menu appears.

2 Move the mouse ⌖ over **Tile** and then press the left button.

◆ The group windows are tiled.

SHORT CUT

Press Shift + F4

SCROLL THROUGH A WINDOW

Scroll bars appear when a window is not large enough to display all of its icons. To view the rest of these "hidden" icons, you can scroll through the window.

Scroll Down or Up One Line

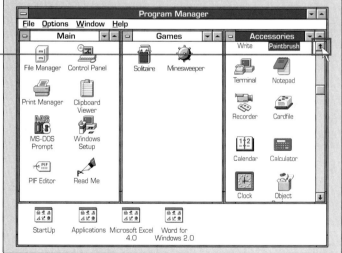

Scroll Down

1 Move the mouse ⟍ over the down scroll arrow and then press the left button.

Scroll Up

1 Move the mouse ⟍ over the up scroll arrow and then press the left button.

Scroll to Any Position

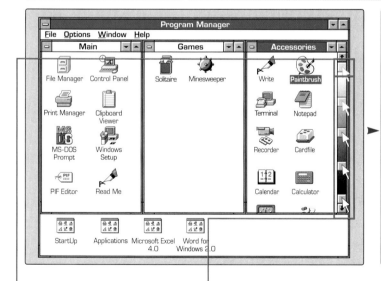

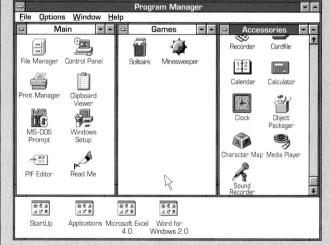

1 To quickly scroll through a window, move the mouse ⟍ over the scroll box and then press and hold down the left button.

2 Still holding down the button, drag the scroll box straight down to the end of the scroll bar.

3 Release the button.

HELP
CONTENTS

You can use the Windows Help feature to learn how to perform a task. This will save you time by eliminating the need to refer to other sources.

Help Contents

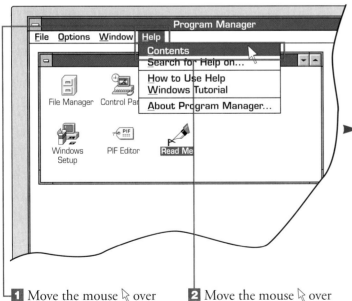

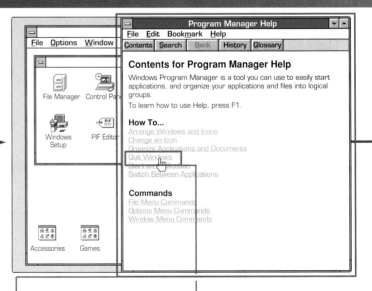

1 Move the mouse ⌖ over **Help** and then press the left button. The **Help** menu appears.

2 Move the mouse ⌖ over **Contents** and then press the left button.

◆ The **Program Manager Help** window appears.

3 Move the mouse ⌖ over a topic of interest (example: Quit Windows) and ⌖ becomes 🖑. Then press the left button.

| Getting Started | Windows Basics | **Help** | Manage Your Applications | Manage Your Directories | Manage Your Files | Manage Your Diskettes | Manage Your Work |

Help Contents
Context Sensitive Help
Search for Help

WINDOWS TUTORIAL

The Windows Tutorial shows you how to use a mouse and explains the basics of the Windows program.

1 To start the tutorial, move the mouse ⌖ over **Help** and then press the left button.

2 Move the mouse ⌖ over **Windows Tutorial** and then press the left button.

To proceed with the **Windows Tutorial**, follow the instructions on your screen.

Help
Contents
Search for Help on...
How to Use Help
Windows Tutorial
About Program Manager...

Welcome to the Microsoft Windows Tutorial.

Press the ESC key to exit the Tutorial.

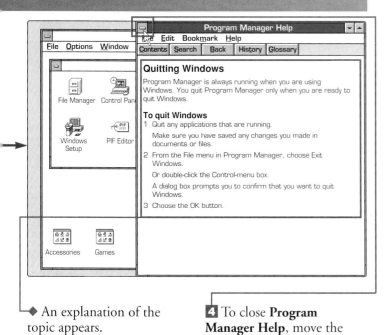

Quitting Windows

Program Manager is always running when you are using Windows. You quit Program Manager only when you are ready to quit Windows.

To quit Windows

1 Quit any applications that are running.

Make sure you have saved any changes you made in documents or files.

2 From the File menu in Program Manager, choose Exit Windows.

Or double-click the Control-menu box.

A dialog box prompts you to confirm that you want to quit Windows.

3 Choose the OK button.

◆ An explanation of the topic appears.

4 To close **Program Manager Help**, move the mouse ⌖ over its **control-menu box** and then quickly press the left button twice.

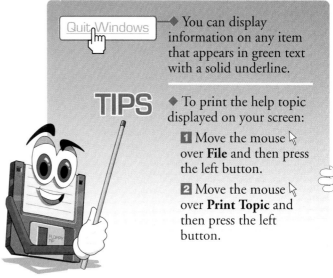

◆ You can display information on any item that appears in green text with a solid underline.

TIPS

◆ To print the help topic displayed on your screen:

1 Move the mouse ⌖ over **File** and then press the left button.

2 Move the mouse ⌖ over **Print Topic** and then press the left button.

CONTEXT SENSITIVE HELP

You can receive detailed help information on any command or dialog box.

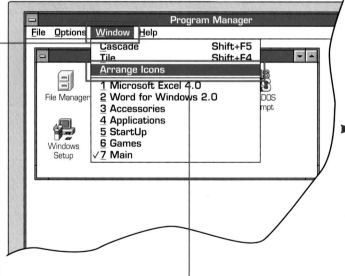

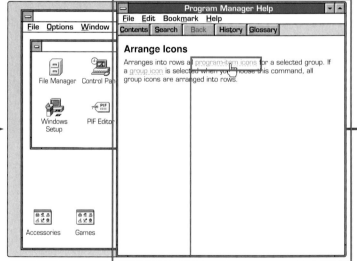

1 Move the mouse ⬚ over a menu name (example: **Window**) and then press the left button. A menu appears.

2 Press ⬇ on your keyboard until you highlight the command you want help on (example: **Arrange Icons**).

3 Press **F1** and the **Program Manager Help** window appears displaying information about the command.

4 To display a definition of a term on your screen (example: program-item icons), move the mouse ⬚ over the term and ⬚ becomes ⬚. Then press the left button.

INTRODUCTION TO WINDOWS

| Getting Started | Windows Basics | **Help** | Manage Your Applications | Manage Your Directories | Manage Your Files | Manage Your Diskettes | Manage Your Work |

Help Contents
Context Sensitive Help
Search for Help

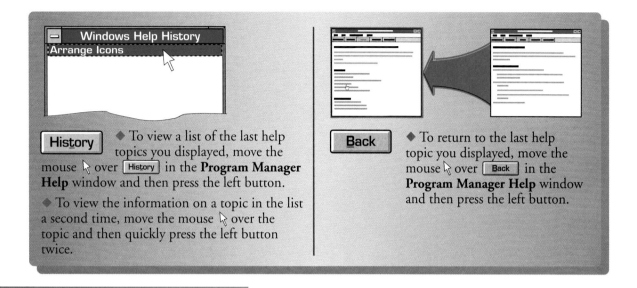

History ◆ To view a list of the last help topics you displayed, move the mouse over `History` in the **Program Manager Help** window and then press the left button.

◆ To view the information on a topic in the list a second time, move the mouse over the topic and then quickly press the left button twice.

Back ◆ To return to the last help topic you displayed, move the mouse over `Back` in the **Program Manager Help** window and then press the left button.

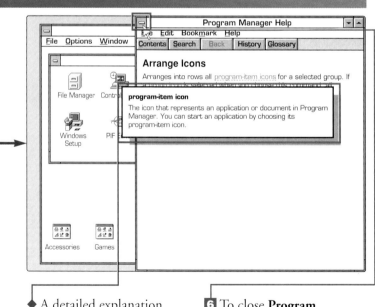

◆ A detailed explanation of the term appears.

5 To remove the explanation, press the left button.

6 To close **Program Manager Help**, move the mouse over its **control-menu box** and then quickly press the left button twice.

TIP

◆ You can display a definition of any term that appears in green text with a dotted underline.

SEARCH FOR HELP

You can search for help information on a specific topic. Windows will locate and display the information.

Search for Help on a Specific Topic

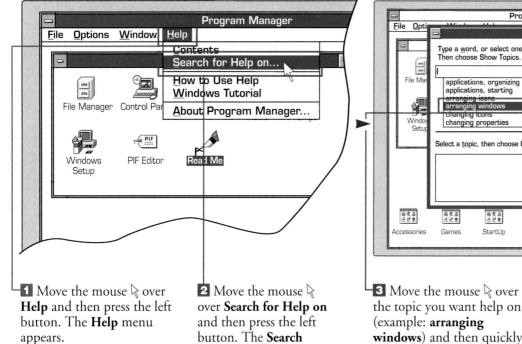

1 Move the mouse ⬚ over **Help** and then press the left button. The **Help** menu appears.

2 Move the mouse ⬚ over **Search for Help on** and then press the left button. The **Search** dialog box appears.

3 Move the mouse ⬚ over the topic you want help on (example: **arranging windows**) and then quickly press the left button twice.

◆ To view more topics, move the mouse ⬚ over the down scroll arrow ⬇ and then press the left button.

INTRODUCTION TO WINDOWS

| Getting Started | Windows Basics | **Help** | Manage Your Applications | Manage Your Directories | Manage Your Files | Manage Your Diskettes | Manage Your Work |

Help Contents
Context Sensitive Help
Search for Help

GLOSSARY

If you want to know the meaning of a word, you can use the Windows Help Glossary to display a definition.

1 To display the Glossary, move the mouse ⤢ over `Glossary` in the **Program Manager Help** window and then press the left button.

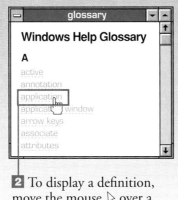

2 To display a definition, move the mouse ⤢ over a word (example: **application**) and ⤢ becomes 🖑. Then press the left button.

◆ A detailed explanation of the word appears.

3 To remove the definition, press the left button.

4 To close the **Glossary**, move the mouse ⤢ over its **control-menu box** and then quickly press the left button twice.

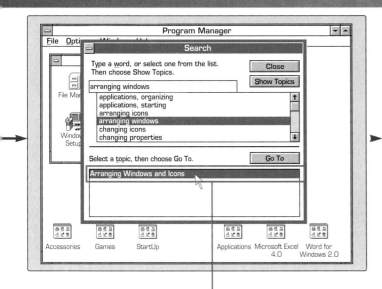

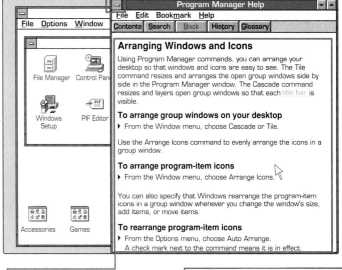

◆ A list of the available topics in the category appears.

Note: In this example, only one topic is displayed.

4 Move the mouse ⤢ over the topic of interest (example: **Arranging Windows and Icons**) and then quickly press the left button twice.

◆ Information on the selected topic appears.

5 To close **Program Manager Help**, move the mouse ⤢ over its **control-menu box** and then quickly press the left button twice.

*Note: You can also access the **Search** dialog box by moving the mouse ⤢ over `Search` and then pressing the left button.*

START
APPLICATIONS

> Applications enable you to perform many different tasks on your computer. They help you write letters, sort information, draw pictures and even play games.

Start Applications

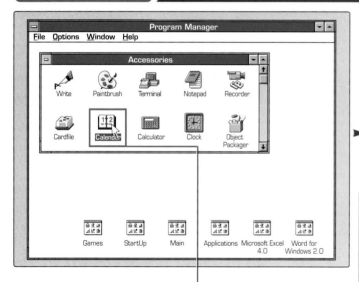

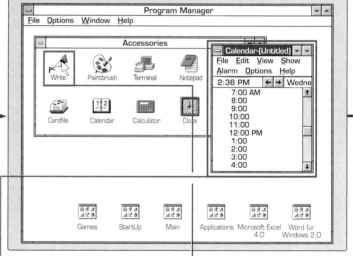

Windows enables you to work with several applications at the same time.

1 To start an application, move the mouse ⃕ over its icon (example: **Calendar**) and then quickly press the left button twice.

2 Size and move the window as shown above. This provides more room on your screen for any other applications you wish to start.

Note: To size a window, refer to page 14. To move a window, refer to page 12.

3 To start another application, move the mouse ⃕ over its icon (example: **Write**) and then quickly press the left button twice.

*Note: Some open applications may become hidden behind the **Program Manager** window (example: **Calendar**).*

INTRODUCTION TO WINDOWS

| Getting Started | Windows Basics | Help | **Manage Your Applications** | Manage Your Directories | Manage Your Files | Manage Your Diskettes | Manage Your Work |

Start Applications
Switch Between Applications
Cascade Application Windows
Tile Application Windows
Arrange Application Icons
Close an Application

You can reduce an application to an icon to provide more room for other applications on your desktop. The application is still in electronic memory, enabling you to instantly access it.

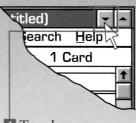

1 To reduce an application to an icon, move the mouse ⌐ over its **Minimize** button and then press the left button.

2 To restore a minimized application to a window, move the mouse ⌐ over its icon and then quickly press the left button twice.

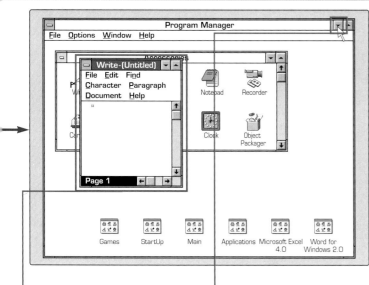

4 Size and move the window as shown above.

5 To start another application (example: **Cardfile**), repeat steps **1** and **2**.

6 To reduce the **Program Manager** window to an icon, move the mouse ⌐ over its **Minimize** button and then press the left button.

◆ The **Program Manager** is reduced to an icon. This clears your screen so you can view the other applications.

◆ The active application displays a blue title bar (example: **Cardfile**). You can only work with the active application.

SWITCH BETWEEN APPLICATIONS

If you have several applications open, some of them may be hidden. Switching between your applications enables you to view each one in turn.

Switch Between Applications (Method 1)

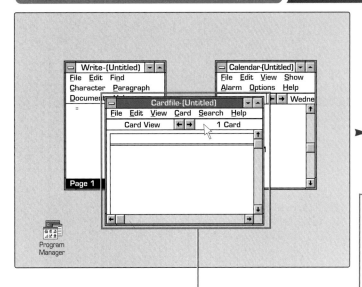

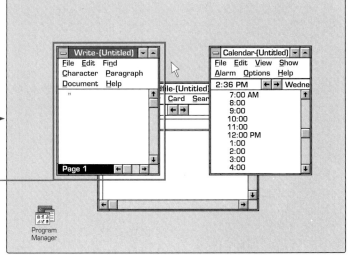

This method is useful if you only have a few applications open.

◆ The active application displays a blue title bar (example: **Cardfile**).

Note: You can only add or edit information in the active application.

1 Press `Alt` + `Esc` until the application you want to switch to becomes active (example: **Write**).

SHORT CUT

To make an application active, move the mouse anywhere over its window and then press the left button.

INTRODUCTION TO WINDOWS

| Getting Started | Windows Basics | Help | **Manage Your Applications** | Manage Your Directories | Manage Your Files | Manage Your Diskettes | Manage Your Work |

SWITCH BETWEEN APPLICATIONS (METHOD 3)

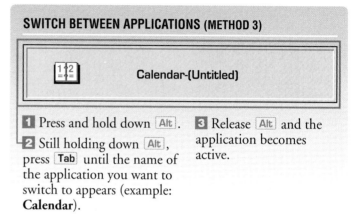

Calendar-(Untitled)

1 Press and hold down `Alt`.

2 Still holding down `Alt`, press `Tab` until the name of the application you want to switch to appears (example: **Calendar**).

3 Release `Alt` and the application becomes active.

Switch Between Applications (Method 2)

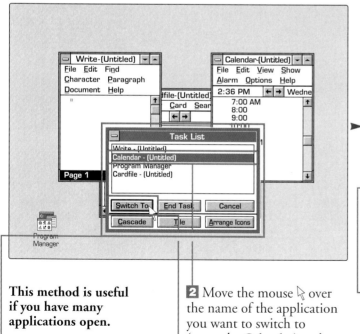

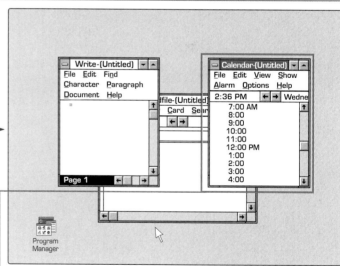

This method is useful if you have many applications open.

1 Press `Ctrl` + `Esc` and the **Task List** dialog box appears.

2 Move the mouse ▷ over the name of the application you want to switch to (example: **Calendar**) and then press the left button.

3 Move the mouse ▷ over **Switch To** and then press the left button.

◆ The application window (example: **Calendar**) moves to the front and becomes the active window.

SHORTCUT

To display the **Task List** dialog box, move the mouse ▷ over any area on your screen not covered by a window and then quickly press the left button twice.

CASCADE APPLICATION WINDOWS

TILE APPLICATION WINDOWS

If you have several application windows open, some of them may be hidden from view. The Cascade command enables you to display all of your open application windows by overlapping them.

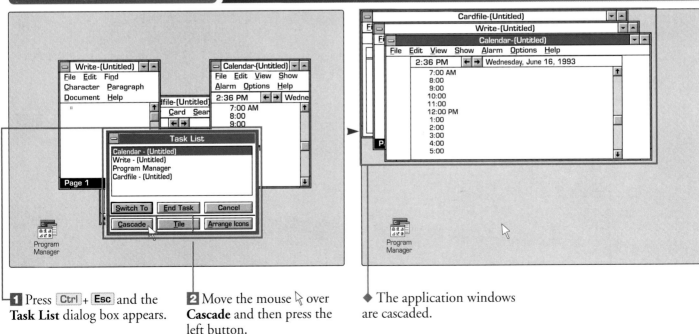

1 Press **Ctrl** + **Esc** and the **Task List** dialog box appears.

2 Move the mouse ⟍ over **Cascade** and then press the left button.

◆ The application windows are cascaded.

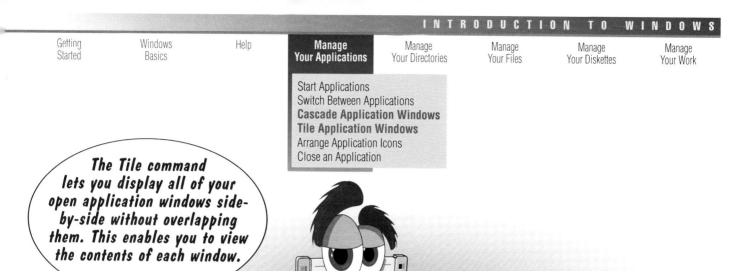

Getting
Started

Windows
Basics

Help

**Manage
Your Applications**

Manage
Your Directories

Manage
Your Files

Manage
Your Diskettes

Manage
Your Work

Start Applications
Switch Between Applications
Cascade Application Windows
Tile Application Windows
Arrange Application Icons
Close an Application

The Tile command lets you display all of your open application windows side-by-side without overlapping them. This enables you to view the contents of each window.

Tile Application Windows

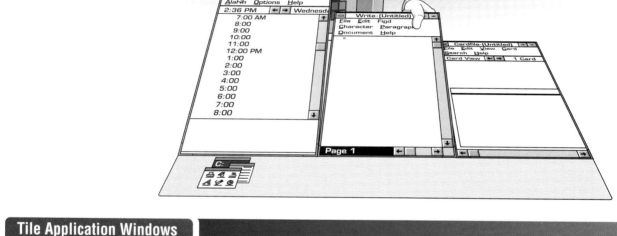

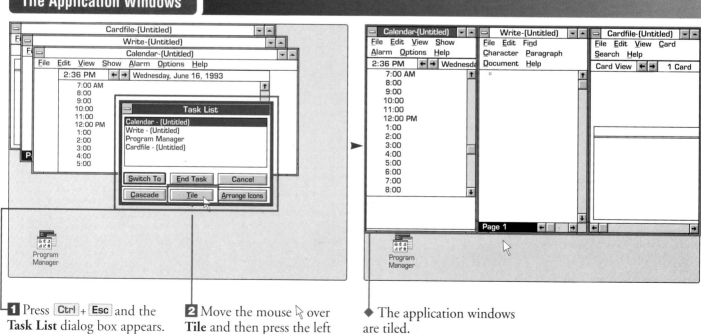

1 Press `Ctrl` + `Esc` and the **Task List** dialog box appears.

2 Move the mouse ⬚ over **Tile** and then press the left button.

◆ The application windows are tiled.

ARRANGE APPLICATION ICONS

CLOSE AN APPLICATION

If your application icons are scattered around your screen, you can use the Arrange Icons feature to line them up in an orderly fashion.

Arrange Application Icons

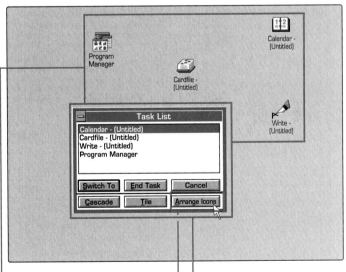

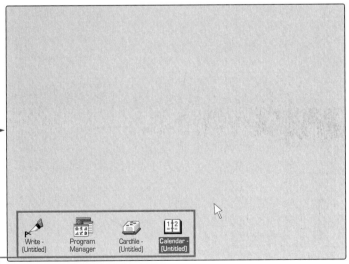

◆ In this example, reduce the applications to icons and then move them as shown above.

Note: To reduce an application to an icon, refer to page 37. To move an icon, refer to page 16.

1 Press **Ctrl** + **Esc** and the **Task List** dialog box appears.

2 Move the mouse ▷ over **Arrange Icons** and then press the left button.

◆ The application icons are neatly arranged along the bottom of your screen.

Note: To restore an application to a window, move the mouse ▷ over its icon and then quickly press the left button twice.

| Getting
Started | Windows
Basics | Help | **Manage
Your Applications** | Manage
Your Directories | Manage
Your Files | Manage
Your Diskettes | Manage
Your Work |

Start Applications
Switch Between Applications
Cascade Application Windows
Tile Application Windows
Arrange Application Icons
Close an Application

Closing an application tells Windows you have completed a task. This will make room for other applications you want to use.

Close an Application

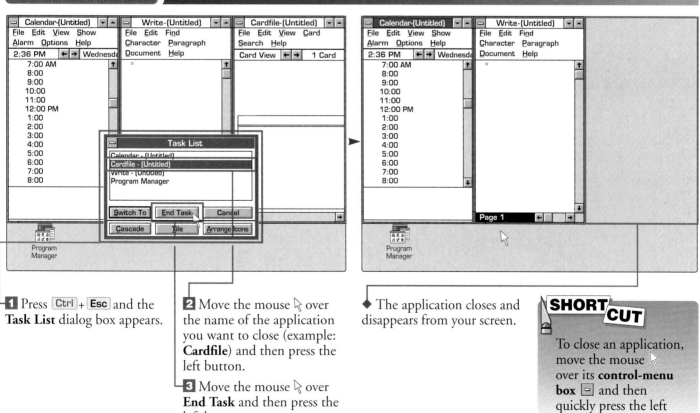

1 Press `Ctrl` + `Esc` and the **Task List** dialog box appears.

2 Move the mouse ▷ over the name of the application you want to close (example: **Cardfile**) and then press the left button.

3 Move the mouse ▷ over **End Task** and then press the left button.

◆ The application closes and disappears from your screen.

SHORTCUT

To close an application, move the mouse ▷ over its **control-menu box** ⊟ and then quickly press the left button twice.

INTRODUCTION

What the File Manager can do for You

In a traditional office, you can use filing cabinets to store and retrieve your documents. This keeps your information organized and manageable.

Windows includes a powerful program called the File Manager. This program functions like an electronic office, providing ways to organize and manage documents stored on your computer.

◆ The File Manager enables you to instantly find, sort, copy, move, delete and view your documents (or files).

◆ You can create new folders (or directories) to help you organize the information stored on your computer.

◆ You can use the File Manager to store data on diskettes. This provides a convenient way to transfer data to other computers or backup important information.

INTRODUCTION TO WINDOWS

| Getting Started | Windows Basics | Help | Manage Your Applications | **Manage Your Directories** | Manage Your Files | Manage Your Diskettes | Manage Your Work |

What are Drives?

Your computer stores programs and data in devices called "drives." Like a filing cabinet, a drive stores information in an organized way.

◆ Most computers have one hard drive and one or two floppy drives. The hard drive is called drive **C**. The floppy drives are called drives **A** and **B**.

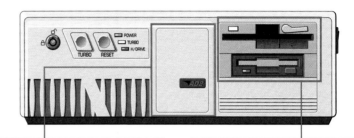

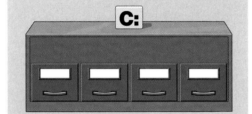

Hard drive (C:)

◆ A hard drive permanently stores programs and data. Most computers have at least one hard drive, called drive **C**.

*Note: Your computer may be set up to have additional hard drives (example: **drive D**).*

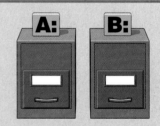

Floppy drives (A: and B:)

◆ A floppy drive stores programs and data on removable diskettes (or floppy disks). A diskette operates slower and stores less data than a hard drive.

Diskettes are used to:
● Load new programs.
● Store backup copies of data.
● Transfer data to other computers.

If your computer has only one floppy drive, it is called drive **A**.

If your computer has two floppy drives, the second drive is called drive **B**.

TIP

DRIVE NAME

A: ◆ A drive name consists of two parts: the letter and a colon (:). The colon represents the word "drive." For example, **A:** refers to the **A drive**.

What are Directories?

Directories are like the drawers and folders in a filing cabinet. They help you organize the programs and data stored in the drives.

Root directory

◆ **Root directory**

The main directory is called the root directory. All other directories are located below this directory.

Note: The \ symbol by itself stands for the root directory.

◆ **Directories**

A directory usually contains related information. For example, the **DATA** directory contains all your data files.

◆ **Files**

A file is a document you name and save. It is stored in a directory.

INTRODUCTION TO WINDOWS

| Getting Started | Windows Basics | Help | Manage Your Applications | **Manage Your Directories** | Manage Your Files | Manage Your Diskettes | Manage Your Work |

What is a Path?

IN EVERYDAY LANGUAGE

To locate the MERGE.LET file, you must:

Find the cabinet labeled **C:** and then

Go to the drawer labeled **DATA** and then

Go to the folder labeled **WPDATA** and then

Go to the file labeled **MERGE.LET**

Go to **equals** \

IN COMPUTER LANGUAGE

To retrieve the MERGE.LET file, replace the words Go to with \. Type the following:

C:\DATA\WPDATA\MERGE.LET

OPEN THE
FILE MANAGER

1 To open the **File Manager**, move the mouse ⃕ over its icon and then quickly press the left button twice.

The File Manager helps you organize and manage your files and directories.

Program Manager

File   Options   Window   Help

Main

File Manager   Control Panel   Print Manager   Clipboard Viewer   MS-DOS Prompt

Windows Setup   PIF Editor   Read Me

Accessories   ...hes   StartUp   Applications   Microsoft Excel 4.0   Word for Windows 2.0

POWER
TURBO
H/DRIVE

TURBO   RESET

AD2

Num Lock   Caps Lock   Scroll Lock

◆ DRIVE ICONS

Windows represents each floppy and hard drive on your computer as an icon and drive letter. The outlined icon is the current drive (example: **drive c**).

◆ DIRECTORY PATH

The directory path displays the location of the current directory.

◆ VOLUME LABEL

You can assign a name to each drive on your computer. The volume label name appears within the [ ] brackets (example: **HARDDRIVE**). Naming the drives is optional.

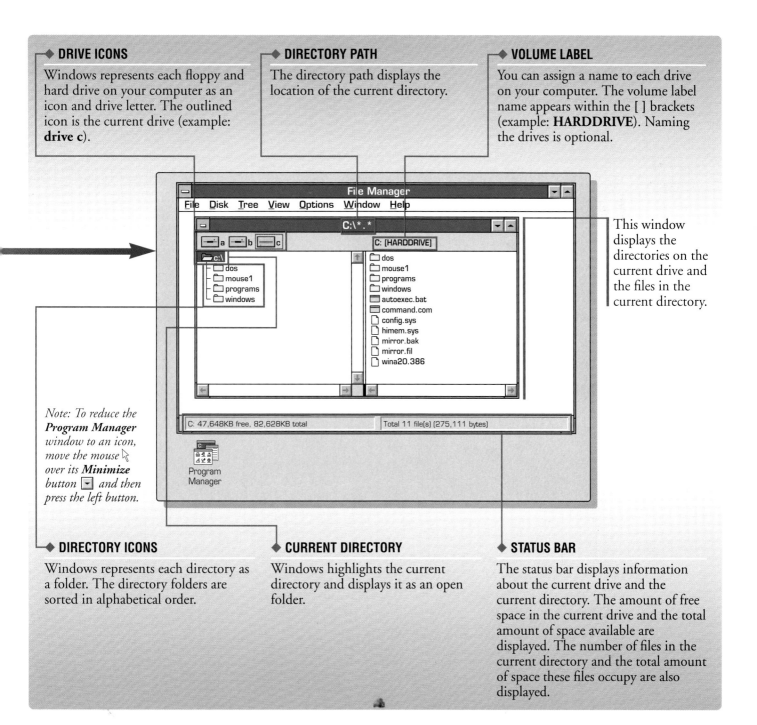

This window displays the directories on the current drive and the files in the current directory.

Note: To reduce the **Program Manager** *window to an icon, move the mouse ⌖ over its* **Minimize** *button* ▾ *and then press the left button.*

◆ DIRECTORY ICONS

Windows represents each directory as a folder. The directory folders are sorted in alphabetical order.

◆ CURRENT DIRECTORY

Windows highlights the current directory and displays it as an open folder.

◆ STATUS BAR

The status bar displays information about the current drive and the current directory. The amount of free space in the current drive and the total amount of space available are displayed. The number of files in the current directory and the total amount of space these files occupy are also displayed.

CHANGE THE SCREEN FONT

A font refers to the design and size of the characters on your screen.

You can change the screen font to suit your needs. For example, if the text is too small, you can increase its size.

Change the Screen Font

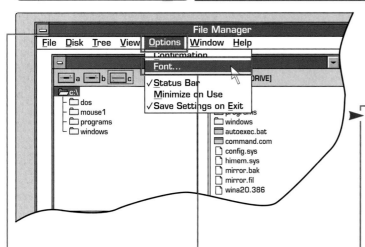

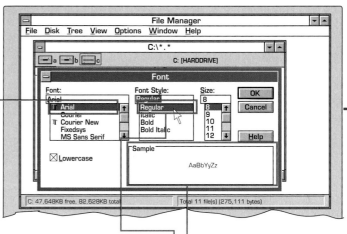

1 Move the mouse ⬚ over **Options** and then press the left button. The **Options** menu appears.

*Assumption: The **File Manager** is open. To open the **File Manager**, refer to page 48.*

2 Move the mouse ⬚ over **Font** and then press the left button.

3 Move the mouse ⬚ over the font you want to use (example: **Arial**) and then press the left button.

Note: To view more fonts, move the mouse ⬚ over the up ⬆ or down ⬇ scroll arrow and then press the left button.

◆ A sample of the font appears in the **Sample** box. The sample changes as you select different font options.

4 Move the mouse ⬚ over the font style you want to use (example: **Regular**) and then press the left button.

I N T R O D U C T I O N   T O   W I N D O W S

| Getting Started | Windows Basics | Help | Manage Your Applications | **Manage Your Directories** | Manage Your Files | Manage Your Diskettes | Manage Your Work |

Windows offers many different fonts. Some examples are:

Arial

Courier New

Times New Roman

Windows offers four different font styles.

Regular

Italic

Bold

Bold Italic

Windows offers many different font sizes. Some examples are:

8

12

24

36

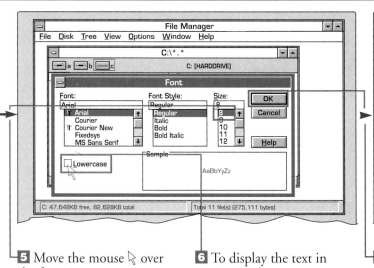

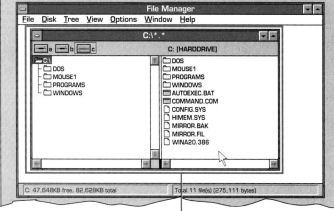

5 Move the mouse ⬁ over the font size you want to use (example: **8**) and then press the left button.

Note: To view more sizes, move the mouse ⬁ over the up ⬆ or down ⬇ scroll arrow and then press the left button.

6 To display the text in uppercase characters, move the mouse ⬁ over the box beside **Lowercase** and then press the left button (⊠ becomes ☐).

*Note: To display the text in lowercase characters, repeat step **6** (☐ becomes ⊠).*

7 Move the mouse ⬁ over **OK** and then press the left button.

◆ The new screen font appears.

*Note: This font will be used in the **File Manager** for the rest of this guide.*

CHANGE DRIVES

 **Change Drives**

If you want to change to a floppy drive, make sure you insert a diskette into the drive.

Note: For more information on floppy drives and diskettes, refer to pages 100 to 102.

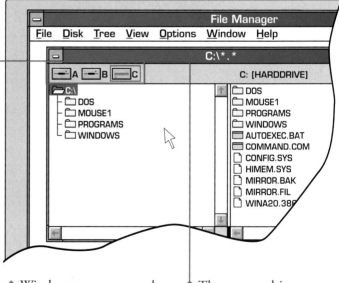

◆ Windows represents each floppy and hard drive on your computer as an icon and drive letter.

◆ The current drive displays a border (example: **drive C**).

*Assumption: The **File Manager** is open. To open the **File Manager**, refer to page 48.*

INTRODUCTION TO WINDOWS

| Getting Started | Windows Basics | Help | Manage Your Applications | **Manage Your Directories** | Manage Your Files | Manage Your Diskettes | Manage Your Work |

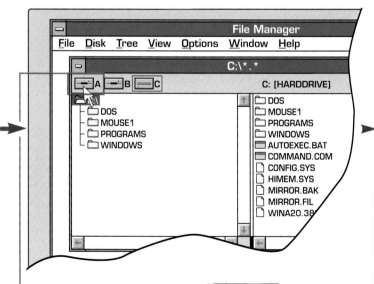

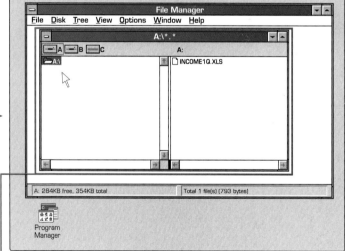

1 To change to another drive, move the mouse ▷ over its icon (example: **drive A**) and then press the left button.

SHORT CUT

To change to another drive, press and hold down Ctrl followed by the drive letter (example: Ctrl + A).

◆ The contents of the drive appear on your screen.

Note: To again display the contents of drive C, move the mouse ▷ over its icon (▭C) and then press the left button.

You can change to another directory to display its contents.

Change Directories

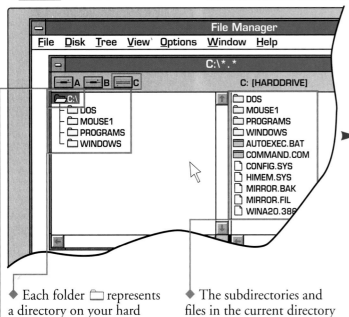

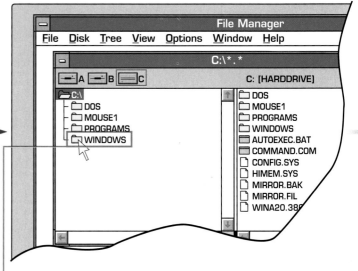

◆ Each folder ⬜ represents a directory on your hard drive.

◆ Windows highlights the current directory and displays it as an open folder (example: **C:**).

◆ The subdirectories and files in the current directory are displayed.

*Assumption: The **File Manager** is open. To open the **File Manager**, refer to page 48.*

1 To change to another directory, move the mouse ⬚ over its folder (example: **WINDOWS**) and then press the left button.

INTRODUCTION TO WINDOWS

| Getting Started | Windows Basics | Help | Manage Your Applications | **Manage Your Directories** | Manage Your Files | Manage Your Diskettes | Manage Your Work |

Introduction
Open the File Manager
Change the Screen Font
Change Drives
Change Directories
Indicate Expandable Branches

Create a Directory
Hide Subdirectories
Display Subdirectories
Move a Directory
Copy a Directory
Delete a Directory

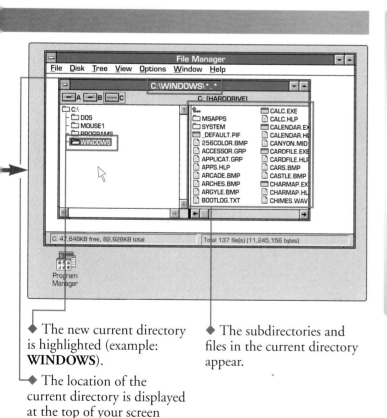

◆ The new current directory is highlighted (example: **WINDOWS**).

◆ The location of the current directory is displayed at the top of your screen (example: **C:\WINDOWS**).

◆ The subdirectories and files in the current directory appear.

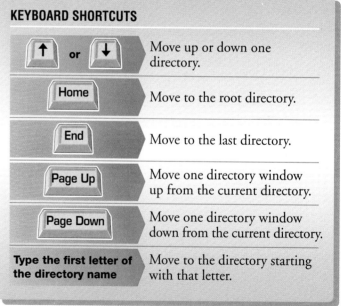

KEYBOARD SHORTCUTS

↑ or ↓	Move up or down one directory.
Home	Move to the root directory.
End	Move to the last directory.
Page Up	Move one directory window up from the current directory.
Page Down	Move one directory window down from the current directory.
Type the first letter of the directory name	Move to the directory starting with that letter.

INDICATE EXPANDABLE BRANCHES

You can quickly see if your directories contain subdirectories by using the Indicate Expandable Branches command.

Indicate Expandable Branches

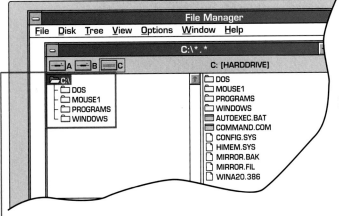

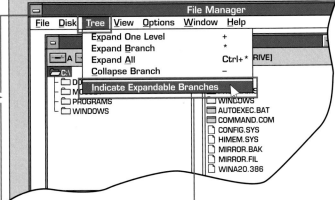

◆ When the **Indicate Expandable Branches** command is **off**, plus (+) and minus (–) signs are not displayed in the directory folders.

*Assumption: The **File Manager** is open. To open the **File Manager**, refer to page 48.*

1 To turn on the **Indicate Expandable Branches** command, move the mouse ▷ over **Tree** and then press the left button. The **Tree** menu appears.

*Note: A check mark (✓) in front of **Indicate Expandable Branches** indicates the command is **on**. To leave the command on, press* Alt *to close the **Tree** menu.*

2 To turn the command **on**, move the mouse ▷ over **Indicate Expandable Branches** and then press the left button.

I N T R O D U C T I O N   T O   W I N D O W S

| Getting Started | Windows Basics | Help | Manage Your Applications | **Manage Your Directories** | Manage Your Files | Manage Your Diskettes | Manage Your Work |

TIP   The **File Manager** takes longer to display a large directory tree when the **Indicate Expandable Branches** command is **on** (as opposed to **off**).

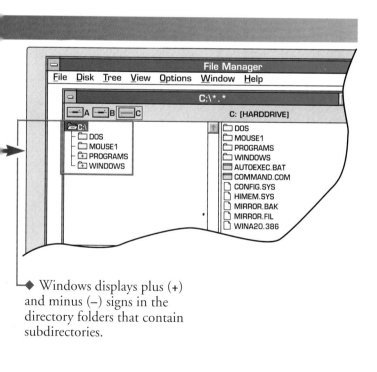

◆ Windows displays plus (+) and minus (–) signs in the directory folders that contain subdirectories.

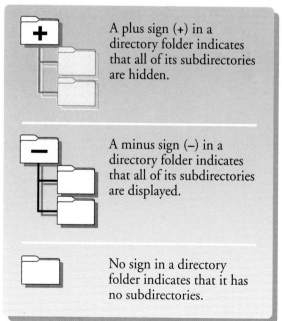

A plus sign (+) in a directory folder indicates that all of its subdirectories are hidden.

A minus sign (–) in a directory folder indicates that all of its subdirectories are displayed.

No sign in a directory folder indicates that it has no subdirectories.

CREATE A DIRECTORY

You can create directories to help you organize the programs and data stored on your hard and floppy drives.

Create a Directory

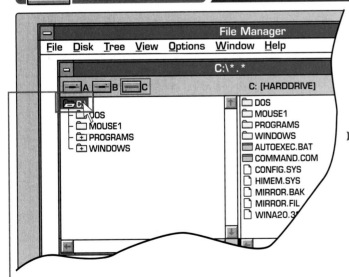

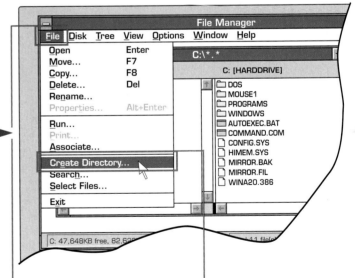

1 To select the directory you want to contain the new directory, move the mouse ⬚ over its name (example: **C:**) and then press the left button.

*Assumption: The **File Manager** is open. To open the **File Manager**, refer to page 48.*

2 Move the mouse ⬚ over **File** and then press the left button. The **File** menu appears.

3 Move the mouse ⬚ over **Create Directory** and then press the left button.

Introduction
Open the File Manager
Change the Screen Font
Change Drives
Change Directories
Indicate Expandable Branches

Create a Directory
Hide Subdirectories
Display Subdirectories
Move a Directory
Copy a Directory
Delete a Directory

All examples in this guide are based on the directory structure illustrated below:

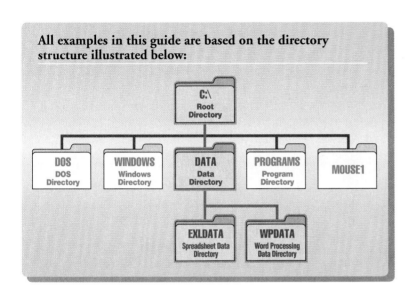

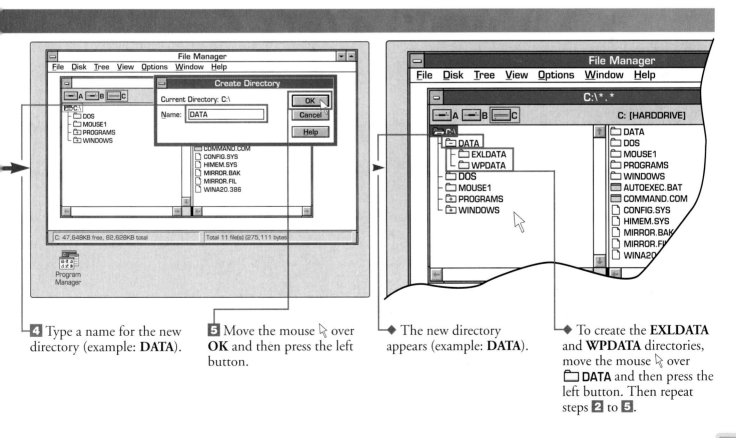

4 Type a name for the new directory (example: **DATA**).

5 Move the mouse ⌖ over **OK** and then press the left button.

◆ The new directory appears (example: **DATA**).

◆ To create the **EXLDATA** and **WPDATA** directories, move the mouse ⌖ over ⌷ **DATA** and then press the left button. Then repeat steps **2** to **5**.

HIDE SUBDIRECTORIES

DISPLAY SUBDIRECTORIES

You can hide all the subdirectories within a directory. This enables you to view directories more clearly by reducing the amount of information on your screen.

Hide Subdirectories

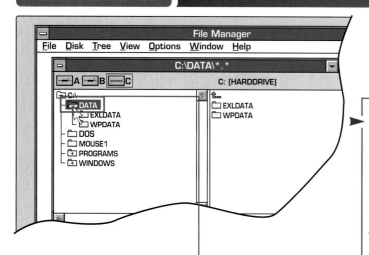

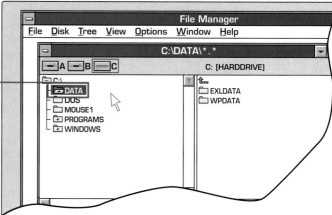

A minus sign (–) in a directory folder indicates that all of its subdirectories are displayed.

Note: To display plus (+) and minus (–) signs in directory folders, refer to page 56.

1 Move the mouse ⬦ over the directory that contains the subdirectories you want to hide (example: **DATA**) and then quickly press the left button twice.

*Assumption: The **File Manager** is open. To open the **File Manager**, refer to page 48.*

◆ All subdirectories in the current directory disappear from your screen.

◆ The directory folder now displays a plus sign (+). This indicates that all of its subdirectories are hidden.

You can display all subdirectories located one level below a directory.

Display Subdirectories (Expand One Level)

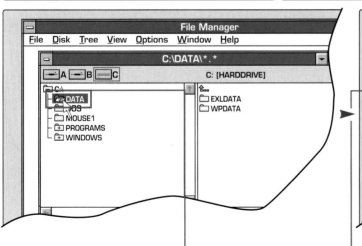

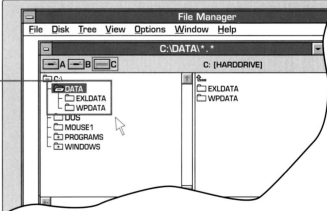

A plus sign (+) in a directory folder indicates that all of its subdirectories are hidden.

1 Move the mouse ⬥ over the directory that contains the subdirectories you want to display (example: **DATA**) and then quickly press the left button twice.

◆ All subdirectories one level below the current directory appear (example: **EXLDATA** and **WPDATA**).

◆ The directory folder now displays a minus sign (–). This indicates that all of its subdirectories are displayed.

Note: For other methods of displaying subdirectories, refer to the next page.

DISPLAY SUBDIRECTORIES

You can display all the subdirectories in a directory or all the subdirectories on your entire drive.

Display Subdirectories (Expand Branch)

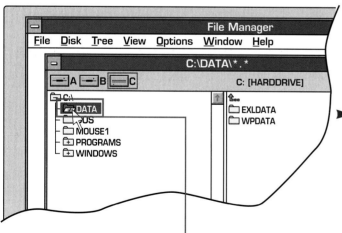

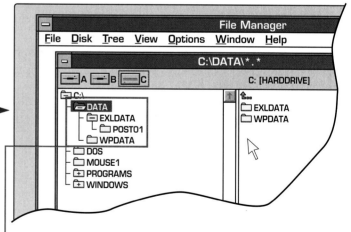

A plus sign (+) in a directory folder indicates that all of its subdirectories are hidden.

Note: To display plus (+) and minus (–) signs in directory folders, refer to page 56.

1 Move the mouse ⌖ over the directory that contains the subdirectories you want to display (example: **DATA**) and then press the left button.

*Assumption: The **File Manager** is open. To open the **File Manager**, refer to page 48.*

2 Press ✱ and all subdirectories in the current directory appear.

◆ The directory folder now displays a minus sign (–). This indicates that all of its subdirectories are displayed.

*Note: The subdirectory **POST01** was created the same way as the **EXLDATA** and **WPDATA** subdirectories. To create a directory, refer to page 58.*

INTRODUCTION TO WINDOWS

| Getting Started | Windows Basics | Help | Manage Your Applications | **Manage Your Directories** | Manage Your Files | Manage Your Diskettes | Manage Your Work |

Display Subdirectories (Expand All)

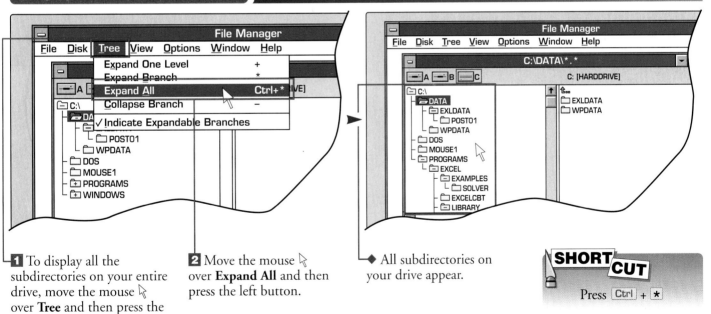

1 To display all the subdirectories on your entire drive, move the mouse ↕ over **Tree** and then press the left button. The **Tree** menu appears.

2 Move the mouse ↕ over **Expand All** and then press the left button.

◆ All subdirectories on your drive appear.

SHORT CUT

Press Ctrl + ✱

MOVE A DIRECTORY

You can move a directory to a new location. The directory is removed from its original place.

Move a Directory (Within the Same Drive)

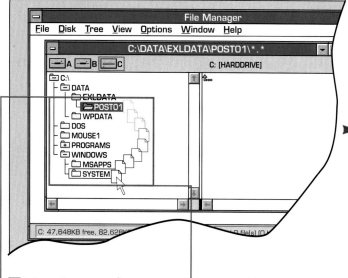

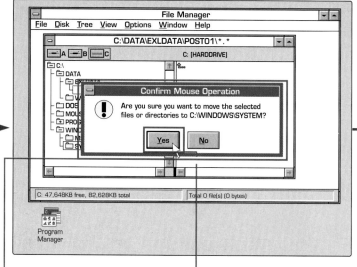

1 Move the mouse ▷ over the directory you want to move (example: **POST01**).

*Assumption: The **File Manager** is open. To open the **File Manager** refer to page 48.*

2 Press and hold down the left button as you drag the directory to a new location. A rectangle appears around the destination directory (example: `SYSTEM`).

3 Release the left button and this dialog box appears.

4 To move the directory, move the mouse ▷ over **Yes** and then press the left button.

*Note: To cancel the move, place the mouse ▷ over **No** and then press the left button.*

Only move directories that you have created for storing data files. Moving a directory containing program files may cause problems (example: do not move the **WINDOWS** directory).

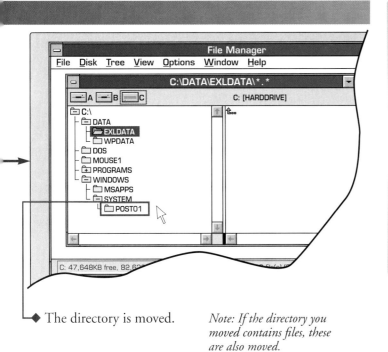

◆ The directory is moved.

Note: If the directory you moved contains files, these are also moved.

MOVE A DIRECTORY (TO A DIFFERENT DRIVE)

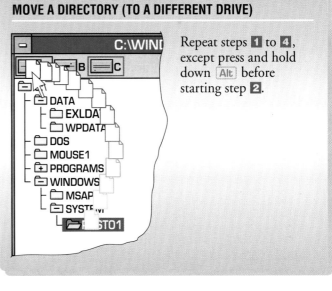

Repeat steps **1** to **4**, except press and hold down Alt before starting step **2**.

COPY A DIRECTORY

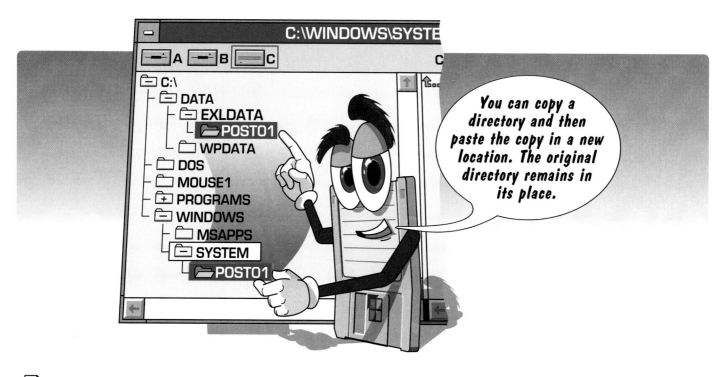

You can copy a directory and then paste the copy in a new location. The original directory remains in its place.

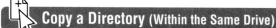

Copy a Directory (Within the Same Drive)

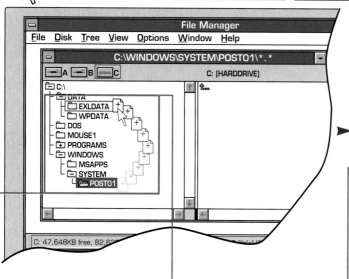

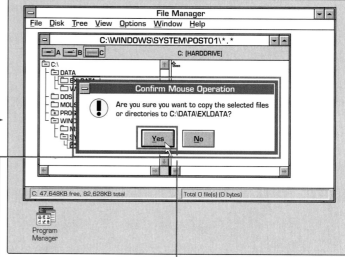

1 Move the mouse ⬦ over the directory you want to copy (example: **POST01**).

*Assumption: The **File Manager** is open. To open the **File Manager**, refer to page 48.*

2 Press and hold down Ctrl.

3 Still holding down Ctrl, press and hold down the left button as you drag the directory to a new location. A rectangle appears around the destination directory (example: 📁EXLDATA).

4 Release the left button and then release Ctrl. This dialog box appears.

5 To copy the directory, move the mouse ⬦ over **Yes** and then press the left button.

*Note: To cancel the copy, move the mouse ⬦ over **No** and then press the left button.*

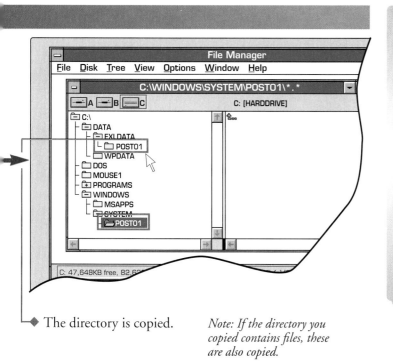

◆ The directory is copied.

Note: If the directory you copied contains files, these are also copied.

COPY A DIRECTORY (TO A DIFFERENT DRIVE)

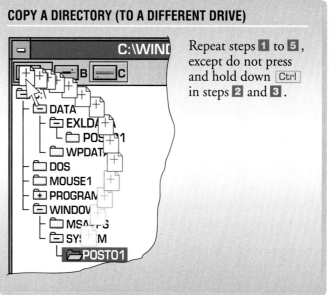

Repeat steps 1 to 5, except do not press and hold down Ctrl in steps 2 and 3.

DELETE A DIRECTORY

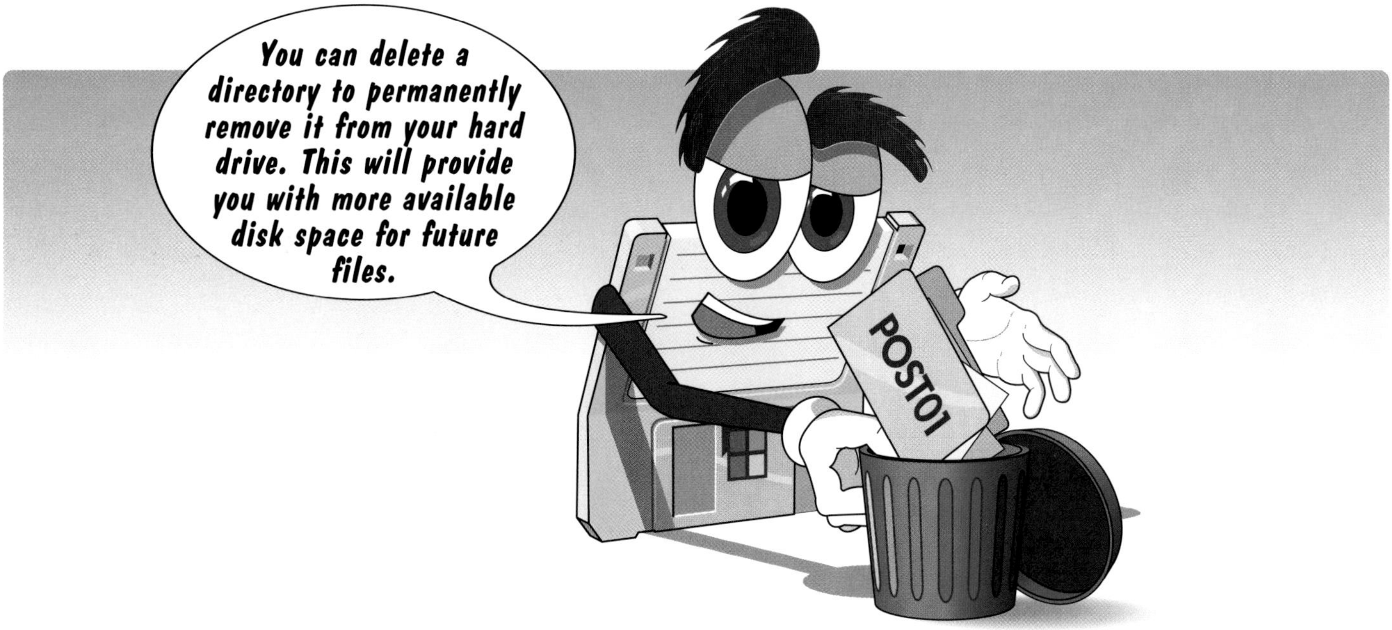
You can delete a directory to permanently remove it from your hard drive. This will provide you with more available disk space for future files.
POST01

Delete a Directory

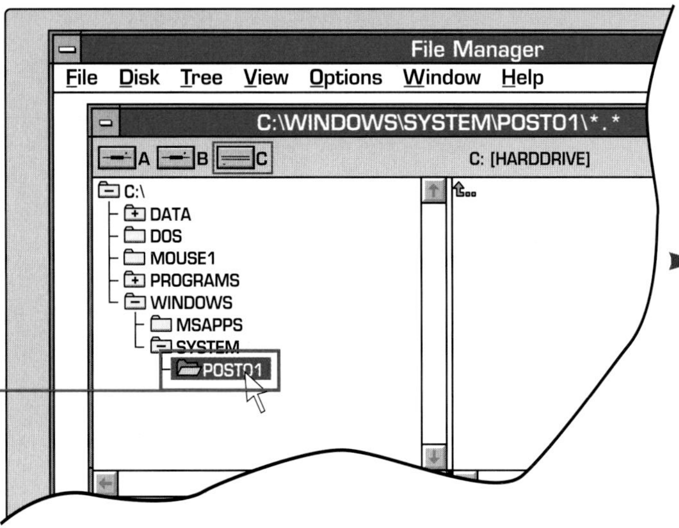
File Manager
File Disk Tree View Options Window Help
C:\WINDOWS\SYSTEM\POST01*.*
A B C
C: [HARDDRIVE]
C:\
DATA
DOS
MOUSE1
PROGRAMS
WINDOWS
MSAPPS
SYSTEM
POST01

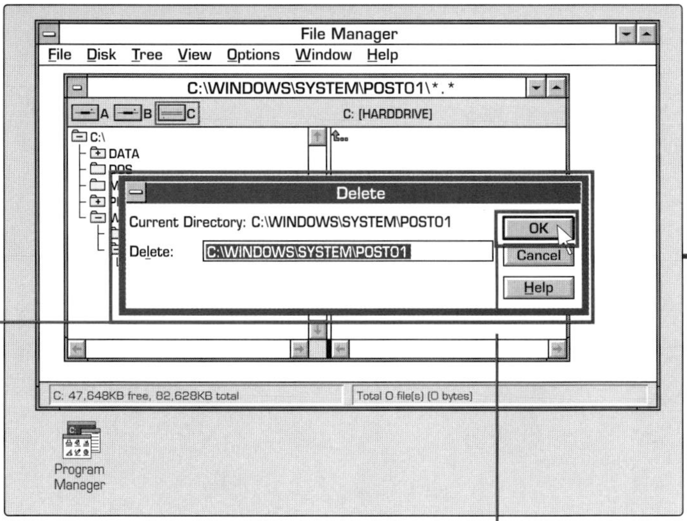
File Manager
File Disk Tree View Options Window Help
C:\WINDOWS\SYSTEM\POST01*.*
A B C
C: [HARDDRIVE]
C:\
DATA
Delete
Current Directory: C:\WINDOWS\SYSTEM\POST01
Delete:
C:\WINDOWS\SYSTEM\POST01
OK
Cancel
Help
C: 47,648KB free, 82,628KB total
Total 0 file(s) (0 bytes)
Program Manager

1 Move the mouse over the directory you want to delete (example: **POST01**) and then press the left button.

*Assumption: The **File Manager** is open. To open the **File Manager**, refer to page 48.*

2 Press Delete and the **Delete** dialog box appears.

3 To delete the directory, move the mouse over **OK** and then press the left button.

*Note: To cancel the deletion, move the mouse over **Cancel** and then press the left button.*

INTRODUCTION TO WINDOWS

| Getting Started | Windows Basics | Help | Manage Your Applications | **Manage Your Directories** | Manage Your Files | Manage Your Diskettes | Manage Your Work |

This dialog box appears if the directory you are deleting contains files.

To delete the directory, you must first delete the files in that directory.

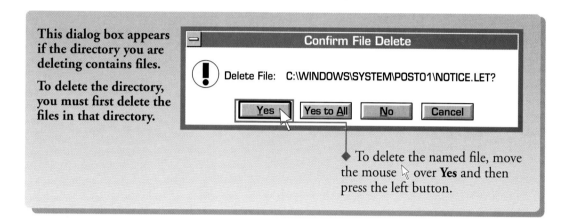

◆ To delete the named file, move the mouse ⌖ over **Yes** and then press the left button.

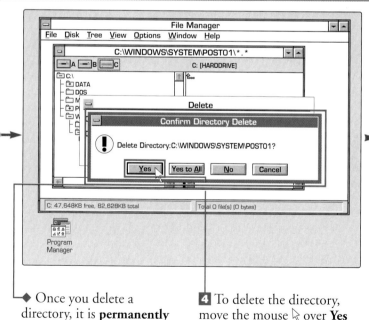

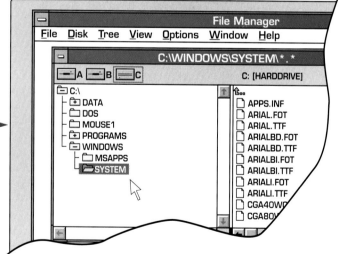

◆ Once you delete a directory, it is **permanently erased** from your drive. This confirmation request offers you a final chance to cancel the deletion.

4 To delete the directory, move the mouse ⌖ over **Yes** and then press the left button.

*Note: If the directory you are deleting contains files, refer to the **Confirm File Delete** dialog box above.*

◆ The directory is deleted from your drive.

INTRODUCTION

What is a File?

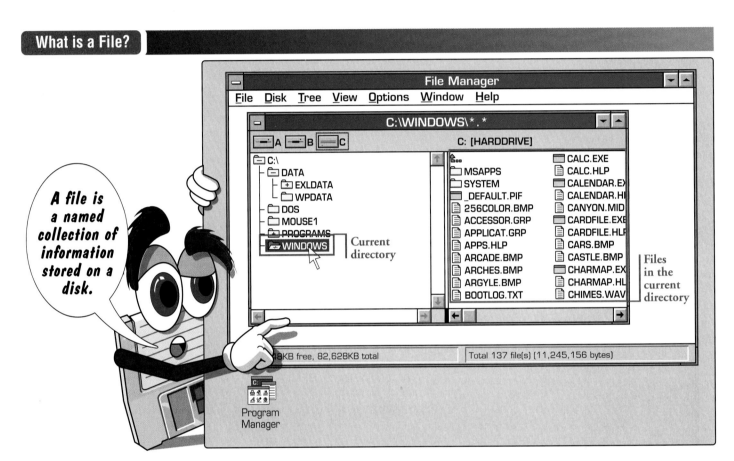

A file is a named collection of information stored on a disk.

Current directory

Files in the current directory

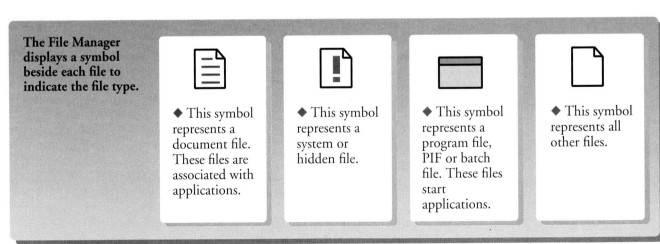

The File Manager displays a symbol beside each file to indicate the file type.

◆ This symbol represents a document file. These files are associated with applications.

◆ This symbol represents a system or hidden file.

◆ This symbol represents a program file, PIF or batch file. These files start applications.

◆ This symbol represents all other files.

INTRODUCTION TO WINDOWS

| Getting Started | Windows Basics | Help | Manage Your Applications | Manage Your Directories | **Manage Your Files** | Manage Your Diskettes | Manage Your Work |

File Names

A file name consists of two parts: a name and an extension. You must separate these parts with a period.

PROJECT3 . WK1

Period
A period must separate the name and the extension.

Name
The name describes the contents of a file. It can have up to 8 characters.

Extension
The extension describes the type of information a file contains. It can have up to 3 characters.

RULES FOR NAMING A FILE

A file name can contain the following characters:

◆ The letters A to Z, upper or lower case

◆ The numbers 0 through 9

◆ The symbols _ ^ $ ~ ! # % & - { } @ ( )

◆ A file name cannot contain a period, blank space or comma

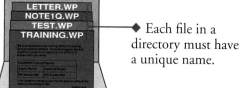

◆ Each file in a directory must have a unique name.

INVALID FILE NAMES

MY WORK.TXT	A file name cannot contain any spaces.
LETTERTOROB.LET	A file name cannot contain more than eight characters before the period.
MEMO\WED.DOC	A file name cannot contain the \ character.

COMMON EXTENSIONS

Word Processing Files

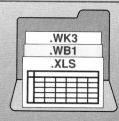

Spreadsheet Files

Program Files

SPLIT A DIRECTORY WINDOW

If there is not enough space to view all your files or directories, you can adjust the size of the display areas.

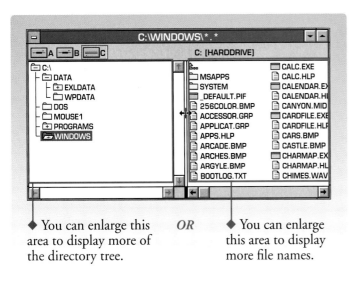

♦ You can enlarge this area to display more of the directory tree.

OR

♦ You can enlarge this area to display more file names.

Split a Directory Window

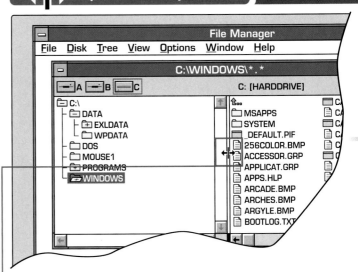

1 Move the mouse ⬚ over the line to the left of the file names and ⬚ changes to ↔.

*Assumption: The **File Manager** is open. To open the **File Manager**, refer to page 48.*

INTRODUCTION TO WINDOWS

| Getting Started | Windows Basics | Help | Manage Your Applications | Manage Your Directories | **Manage Your Files** | Manage Your Diskettes | Manage Your Work |

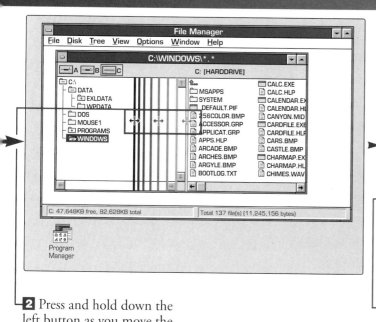

2 Press and hold down the left button as you move the vertical line to a new position.

3 Release the left button and the window splits at the position you specified.

◆ In this example, there is now more space to display the names of the files in the current directory.

TREE AND DIRECTORY VIEWS

You can select one of three different ways to view your directories and files.

Tree and Directory Views

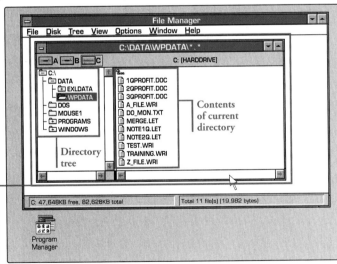

Directory tree

Contents of current directory

C: 47,648KB free, 82,628KB total   Total 11 file(s) (19,982 bytes)

Tree and Directory

◆ This is the initial (or default) setting. Both the directory tree and the contents of the current directory are displayed.

*Assumption: The **File Manager** is open. To open the **File Manager** refer to page 48.*

Directory Only

1 To display only the contents of the current directory, move the mouse over **View** and then press the left button.

2 Move the mouse over **Directory Only** and then press the left button.

INTRODUCTION TO WINDOWS

| Getting Started | Windows Basics | Help | Manage Your Applications | Manage Your Directories | **Manage Your Files** | Manage Your Diskettes | Manage Your Work |

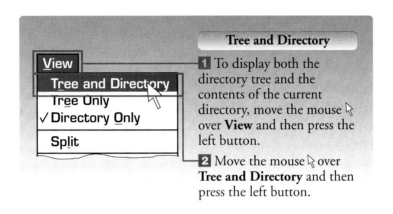

Tree and Directory

1 To display both the directory tree and the contents of the current directory, move the mouse over **View** and then press the left button.

2 Move the mouse over **Tree and Directory** and then press the left button.

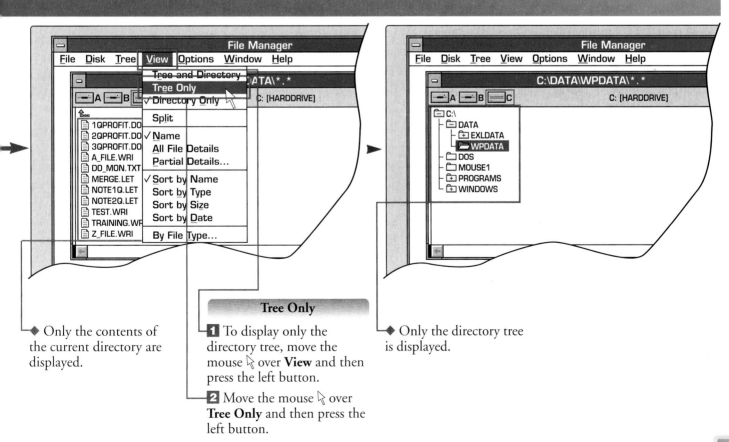

◆ Only the contents of the current directory are displayed.

Tree Only

1 To display only the directory tree, move the mouse over **View** and then press the left button.

2 Move the mouse over **Tree Only** and then press the left button.

◆ Only the directory tree is displayed.

DISPLAY FILE INFORMATION

You can obtain information about the files on your screen. Windows can display the following details:

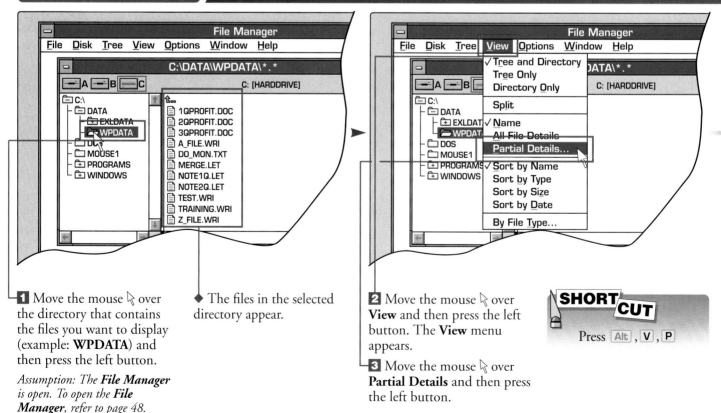

Display File Information

1 Move the mouse � over the directory that contains the files you want to display (example: **WPDATA**) and then press the left button.

*Assumption: The **File Manager** is open. To open the **File Manager**, refer to page 48.*

◆ The files in the selected directory appear.

2 Move the mouse � over **View** and then press the left button. The **View** menu appears.

3 Move the mouse � over **Partial Details** and then press the left button.

SHORT CUT

Press Alt , V , P

INTRODUCTION TO WINDOWS

| Getting Started | Windows Basics | Help | Manage Your Applications | Manage Your Directories | **Manage Your Files** | Manage Your Diskettes | Manage Your Work |

DISPLAY ONLY FILE NAMES

To simplify your screen, you can display the name of each file and hide all other file details.

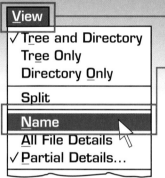

1 Move the mouse ⟍ over **View** and then press the left button.

2 Move the mouse ⟍ over **Name** and then press the left button.

Note: This is the initial (or default) setting.

DISPLAY ALL FILE DETAILS

You can quickly display the following information about each file: name, size, last modification date and time and file attribute status.

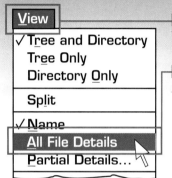

1 Move the mouse ⟍ over **View** and then press the left button.

2 Move the mouse ⟍ over **All File Details** and then press the left button.

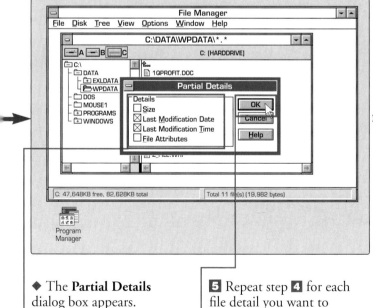

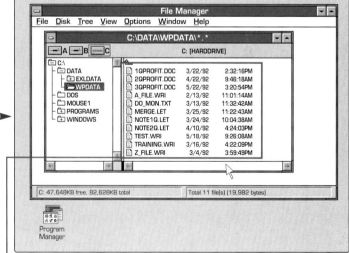

◆ The **Partial Details** dialog box appears.

4 Move the mouse ⟍ over the box beside a file detail you want to display and then press the left button (☐ becomes ☒).

5 Repeat step **4** for each file detail you want to display.

6 Move the mouse ⟍ over **OK** and then press the left button.

◆ Each file now displays the details you selected.

Windows offers four different ways to sort the files displayed on your screen. You can view them by name, type, size or date.

Sort Files

You can sort files by name, type, size or date.

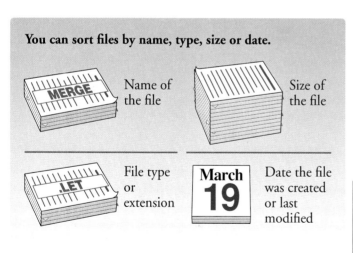

Name of the file

Size of the file

File type or extension

Date the file was created or last modified

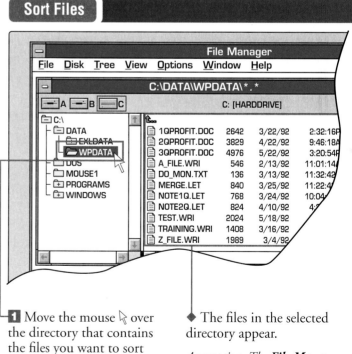

1 Move the mouse � over the directory that contains the files you want to sort (example: **WPDATA**) and then press the left button.

◆ The files in the selected directory appear.

*Assumption: The **File Manager** is open. To open the **File Manager**, refer to page 48.*

INTRODUCTION TO WINDOWS

| Getting Started | Windows Basics | Help | Manage Your Applications | Manage Your Directories | **Manage Your Files** | Manage Your Diskettes | Manage Your Work |

Introduction
Split a Directory Window
Tree and Directory Views
Display File Information
Sort Files
Wildcards

Search for Files
Select Files
Move or Copy Files
Rename a File
Delete Files

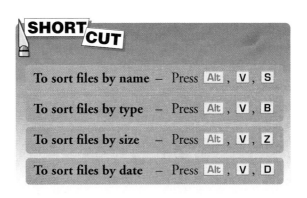

SHORT CUT

To sort files by name – Press `Alt` , `V` , `S`

To sort files by type – Press `Alt` , `V` , `B`

To sort files by size – Press `Alt` , `V` , `Z`

To sort files by date – Press `Alt` , `V` , `D`

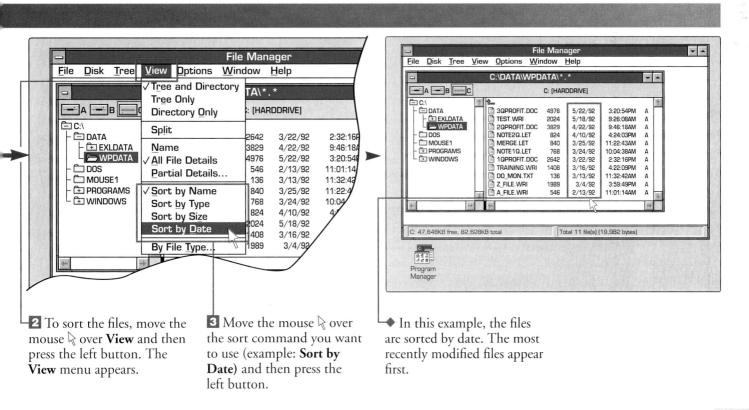

2 To sort the files, move the mouse over **View** and then press the left button. The **View** menu appears.

3 Move the mouse over the sort command you want to use (example: **Sort by Date**) and then press the left button.

◆ In this example, the files are sorted by date. The most recently modified files appear first.

WILDCARDS

Using the ? Wildcard

The question mark (?) represents a single character in a file name.

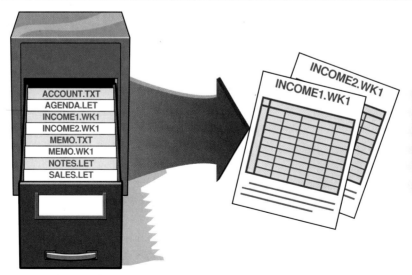

ACCOUNT.TXT
AGENDA.LET
INCOME1.WK1
INCOME2.WK1
MEMO.TXT
MEMO.WK1
NOTES.LET
SALES.LET

INCOME2.WK1
INCOME1.WK1

INCOME?.WK1 includes all files starting with **INCOME**, followed by any single character and then ending with **.WK1**

Note: A file named INCOME1A.WK1 would not be included.

INTRODUCTION TO WINDOWS

Getting Started	Windows Basics	Help	Manage Your Applications	Manage Your Directories	**Manage Your Files**	Manage Your Diskettes	Manage Your Work

Introduction
Split a Directory Window
Tree and Directory Views
Display File Information
Sort Files
Wildcards

Search for Files
Select Files
Move or Copy Files
Rename a File
Delete Files

Using the * Wildcard

The asterisk (*) represents one or more characters in a file name.

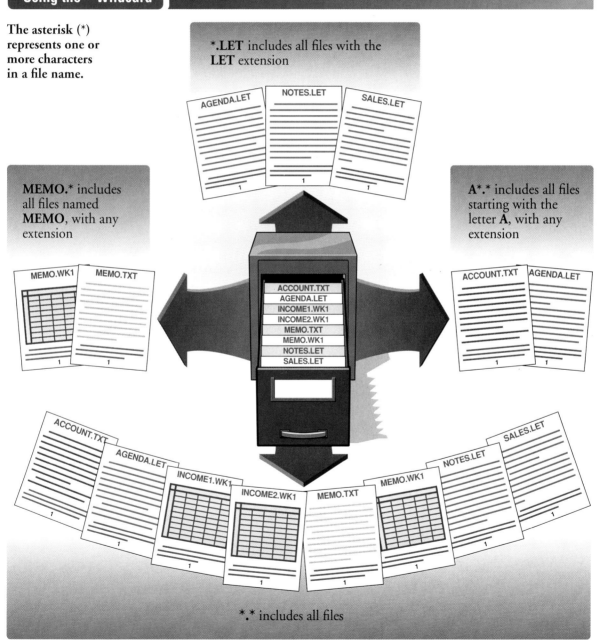

*.LET includes all files with the **LET** extension

AGENDA.LET   NOTES.LET   SALES.LET

MEMO.* includes all files named **MEMO**, with any extension

MEMO.WK1   MEMO.TXT

A*.* includes all files starting with the letter **A**, with any extension

ACCOUNT.TXT   AGENDA.LET

ACCOUNT.TXT
AGENDA.LET
INCOME1.WK1
INCOME2.WK1
MEMO.TXT
MEMO.WK1
NOTES.LET
SALES.LET

ACCOUNT.TXT   AGENDA.LET   INCOME1.WK1   INCOME2.WK1   MEMO.TXT   MEMO.WK1   NOTES.LET   SALES.LET

. includes all files

SEARCH FOR FILES

You can use the Search command to find files on your hard drive. It is not uncommon to forget where you have stored files.

Search for Files

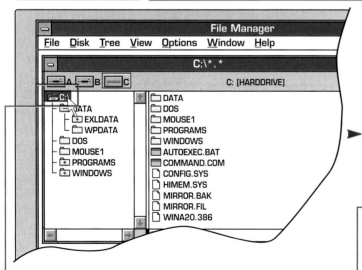

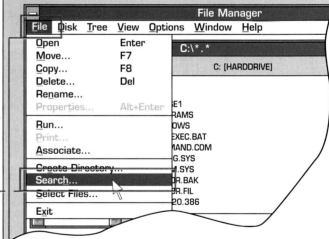

1 Move the mouse ▷ over the directory you want to search (example: **C:**) and then press the left button.

*Assumption: The **File Manager** is open. To open the **File Manager**, refer to page 48.*

◆ Windows will search the current directory and all of its subdirectories.

2 Move the mouse ▷ over **File** and then press the left button. The **File** menu appears.

3 Move the mouse ▷ over **Search** and then press the left button.

Press Alt , F , H

INTRODUCTION TO WINDOWS

| Getting Started | Windows Basics | Help | Manage Your Applications | Manage Your Directories | **Manage Your Files** | Manage Your Diskettes | Manage Your Work |

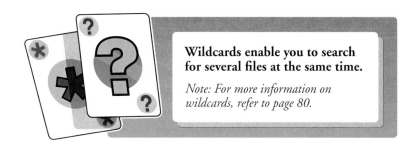

Wildcards enable you to search for several files at the same time.

Note: For more information on wildcards, refer to page 80.

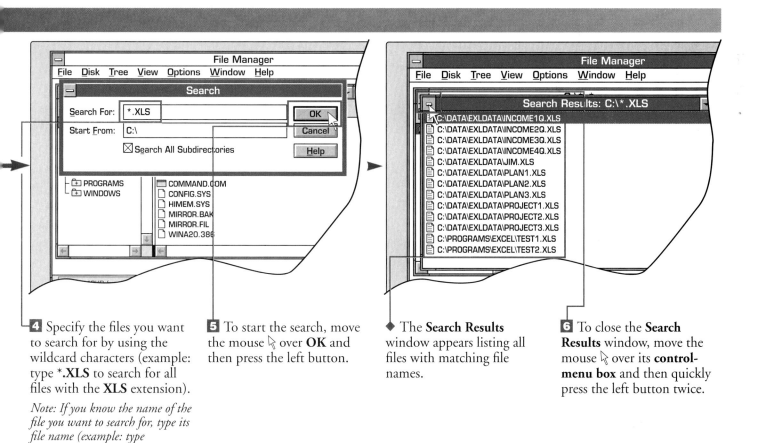

4 Specify the files you want to search for by using the wildcard characters (example: type ***.XLS** to search for all files with the **XLS** extension).

Note: If you know the name of the file you want to search for, type its file name (example: type INCOME1Q.XLS).

5 To start the search, move the mouse ⌕ over **OK** and then press the left button.

◆ The **Search Results** window appears listing all files with matching file names.

6 To close the **Search Results** window, move the mouse ⌕ over its **control-menu box** and then quickly press the left button twice.

SELECT
FILES

To copy, move or delete files, you must first select the files you want to work with. Selected files appear highlighted on your screen.

Select Files Randomly

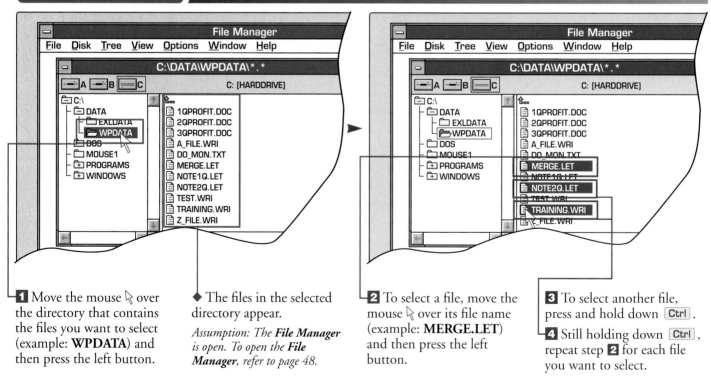

1 Move the mouse � over the directory that contains the files you want to select (example: **WPDATA**) and then press the left button.

◆ The files in the selected directory appear.

*Assumption: The **File Manager** is open. To open the **File Manager**, refer to page 48.*

2 To select a file, move the mouse � over its file name (example: **MERGE.LET**) and then press the left button.

3 To select another file, press and hold down Ctrl.

4 Still holding down Ctrl, repeat step **2** for each file you want to select.

INTRODUCTION TO WINDOWS

| Getting Started | Windows Basics | Help | Manage Your Applications | Manage Your Directories | **Manage Your Files** | Manage Your Diskettes | Manage Your Work |

Introduction
Split a Directory Window
Tree and Directory Views
Display File Information
Sort Files
Wildcards

Search for Files
Select Files
Move or Copy Files
Rename a File
Delete Files

TIPS

◆ To deselect a single file, press and hold down `Ctrl`. Still holding down `Ctrl`, move the mouse ⩗ over the file and then press the left button.

◆ To deselect all the files, move the mouse ⩗ over any file and then press the left button.

Select All Files

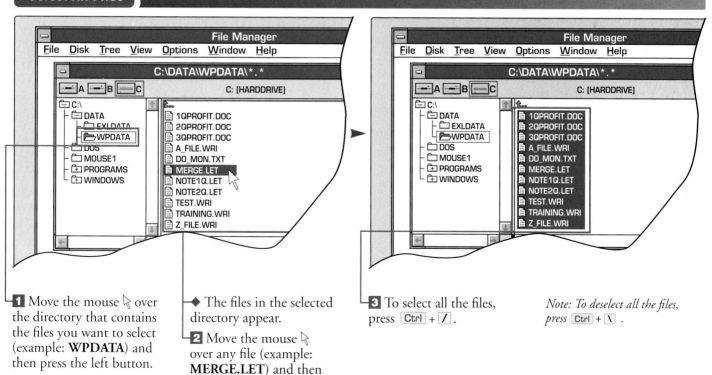

1 Move the mouse ⩗ over the directory that contains the files you want to select (example: **WPDATA**) and then press the left button.

◆ The files in the selected directory appear.

2 Move the mouse ⩗ over any file (example: **MERGE.LET**) and then press the left button.

3 To select all the files, press `Ctrl` + `/`.

Note: To deselect all the files, press `Ctrl` + `\`.

SELECT FILES

Windows lets you select groups of files. This enables you to copy, move or delete several files at the same time. Selected files appear highlighted on your screen.

Select a Group of Files in a Sequence

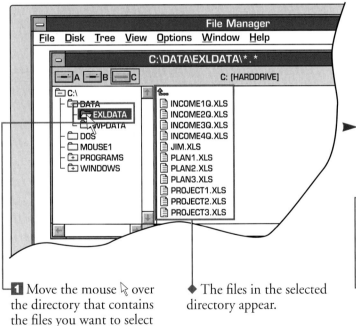

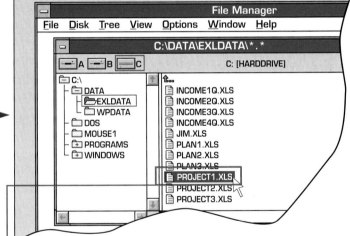

1 Move the mouse ⬚ over the directory that contains the files you want to select (example: **EXLDATA**) and then press the left button.

*Assumption: The **File Manager** is open. To open the **File Manager**, refer to page 48.*

◆ The files in the selected directory appear.

2 To select a group of files, move the mouse ⬚ over the first file you want to select (example: **PROJECT1.XLS**) and then press the left button.

INTRODUCTION TO WINDOWS

| Getting Started | Windows Basics | Help | Manage Your Applications | Manage Your Directories | **Manage Your Files** | Manage Your Diskettes | Manage Your Work |

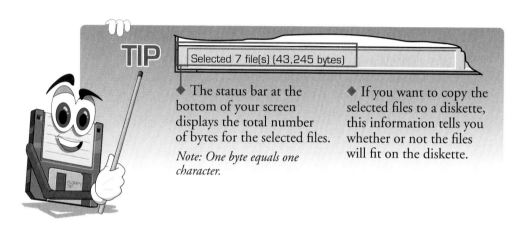

TIP

Selected 7 file(s) (43,245 bytes)

◆ The status bar at the bottom of your screen displays the total number of bytes for the selected files.

Note: One byte equals one character.

◆ If you want to copy the selected files to a diskette, this information tells you whether or not the files will fit on the diskette.

Select Multiple Groups of Files

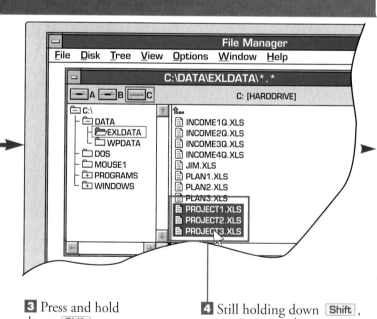

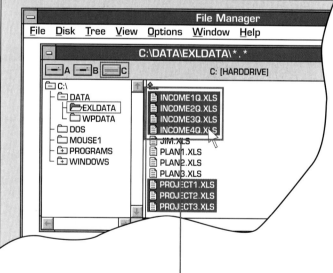

3 Press and hold down Shift.

4 Still holding down Shift, move the mouse ⌖ over the last file in the group (example: **PROJECT3.XLS**) and then press the left button. Release Shift.

5 To select another group of files, press and hold down Ctrl.

6 Still holding down Ctrl, repeat steps **2** to **4**. Do not release Ctrl until you have completed step **4**.

SELECT FILES

Windows enables you to select files with related names all at the same time. You can accomplish this by using the * and ? wildcard characters.

Select Files

File(s): `*.WRI`

Select
Deselect
Close
Help

Select Files Using the Wildcard Characters

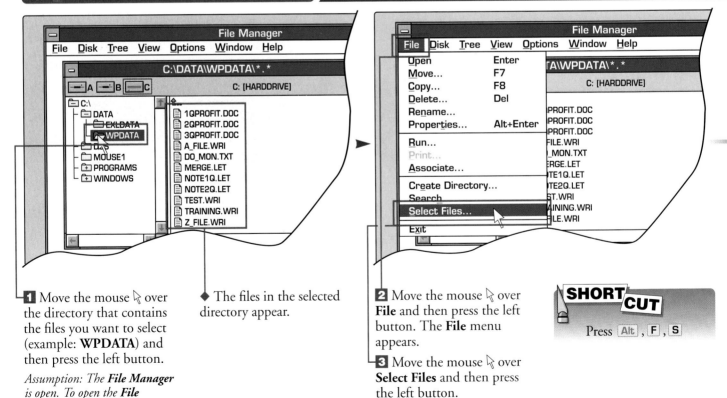

1 Move the mouse ⌖ over the directory that contains the files you want to select (example: **WPDATA**) and then press the left button.

*Assumption: The **File Manager** is open. To open the **File Manager**, refer to page 48.*

◆ The files in the selected directory appear.

2 Move the mouse ⌖ over **File** and then press the left button. The **File** menu appears.

3 Move the mouse ⌖ over **Select Files** and then press the left button.

SHORT CUT

Press `Alt`, `F`, `S`

INTRODUCTION TO WINDOWS

| Getting Started | Windows Basics | Help | Manage Your Applications | Manage Your Directories | **Manage Your Files** | Manage Your Diskettes | Manage Your Work |

TIPS

◆ To deselect a single file, press and hold down Ctrl. Still holding down Ctrl, move the mouse ⌖ over the file and then press the left button.

◆ To deselect all the files, move the mouse ⌖ over any file and then press the left button.

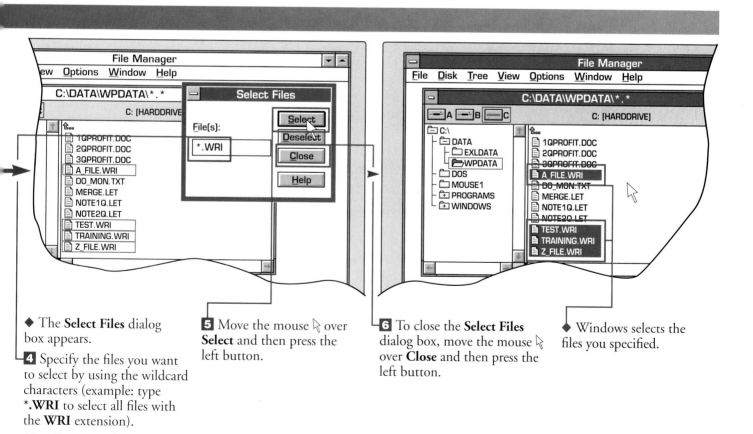

◆ The **Select Files** dialog box appears.

4 Specify the files you want to select by using the wildcard characters (example: type ***.WRI** to select all files with the **WRI** extension).

Note: For more information on wildcards, refer to page 80.

5 Move the mouse ⌖ over **Select** and then press the left button.

6 To close the **Select Files** dialog box, move the mouse ⌖ over **Close** and then press the left button.

◆ Windows selects the files you specified.

MOVE OR COPY FILES

The Move command places exact copies of your files in a new location. Windows deletes the original files. This is helpful if you accidentally stored files in the wrong location.

Move Files (to a Different Directory)

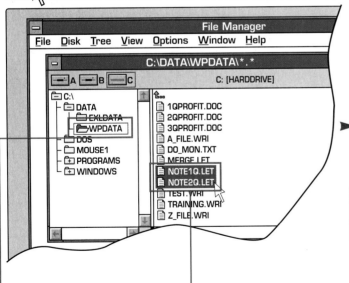

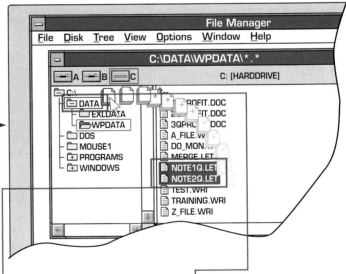

1 Move the mouse ▷ over the directory that contains the files you want to move (example: **WPDATA**) and then press the left button.

*Assumption: The **File Manager** is open. To open the **File Manager**, refer to page 48.*

2 Select the files you want to move to a different directory.

Note: To select files, refer to pages 84 to 89.

3 Move the mouse ▷ over one of the highlighted files and then press and hold down the left button.

4 Still holding down the button, move the mouse ▷ over the directory where you want to move the files (example: **DATA**) and then release the button.

I N T R O D U C T I O N   T O   W I N D O W S

| Getting Started | Windows Basics | Help | Manage Your Applications | Manage Your Directories | **Manage Your Files** | Manage Your Diskettes | Manage Your Work |

Introduction
Split a Directory Window
Tree and Directory Views
Display File Information
Sort Files
Wildcards

Search for Files
Select Files
Move or Copy Files
Rename a File
Delete Files

COPY FILES TO A DIFFERENT DIRECTORY

The Copy command places exact copies of your files in a new location. Windows does not delete the original files.

◆ Repeat steps **1** to **3** below. Then press and hold down [Ctrl] before dragging the files in step **4**.

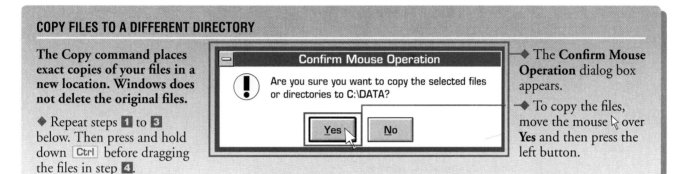

Confirm Mouse Operation

Are you sure you want to copy the selected files or directories to C:\DATA?

Yes   No

◆ The **Confirm Mouse Operation** dialog box appears.

◆ To copy the files, move the mouse ⟩ over **Yes** and then press the left button.

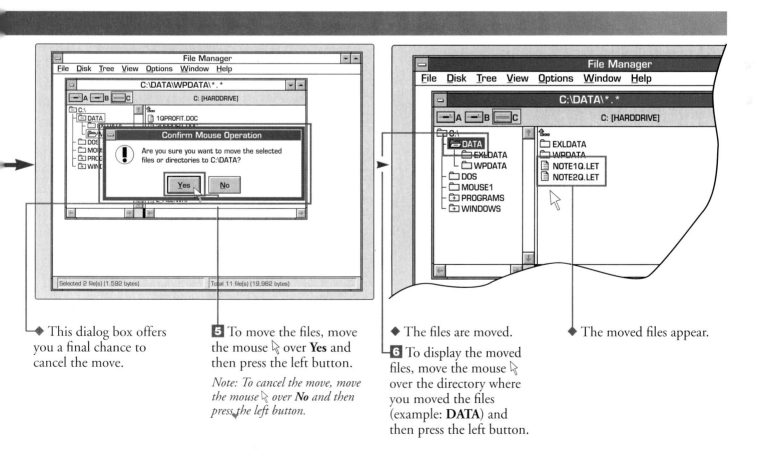

◆ This dialog box offers you a final chance to cancel the move.

5 To move the files, move the mouse ⟩ over **Yes** and then press the left button.

*Note: To cancel the move, move the mouse ⟩ over **No** and then press the left button.*

◆ The files are moved.

6 To display the moved files, move the mouse ⟩ over the directory where you moved the files (example: **DATA**) and then press the left button.

◆ The moved files appear.

MOVE OR
COPY FILES

You can make a copy of a file and place the copy in the same directory. This will enable you to make changes to the file without affecting the original.

Copy a File (Within the Same Directory)

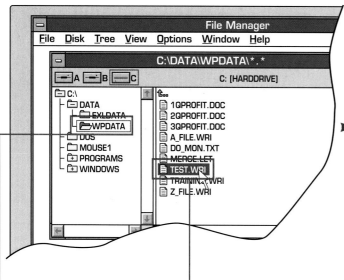

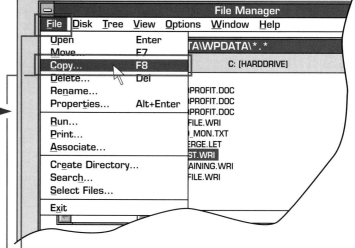

1 Move the mouse ⌖ over the directory that contains the file you want to copy (example: **WPDATA**) and then press the left button.

*Assumption: The **File Manager** is open. To open the **File Manager**, refer to page 48.*

2 To select the file you want to copy, move the mouse ⌖ over the file (example: **TEST.WRI**) and then press the left button.

3 Move the mouse ⌖ over **File** and then press the left button. The **File** menu appears.

4 Move the mouse ⌖ over **Copy** and then press the left button.

Press **F8**

92

INTRODUCTION TO WINDOWS

Getting Started	Windows Basics	Help	Manage Your Applications	Manage Your Directories	**Manage Your Files**	Manage Your Diskettes	Manage Your Work

Introduction	Search for Files
Split a Directory Window	Select Files
Tree and Directory Views	**Move or Copy Files**
Display File Information	Rename a File
Sort Files	Delete Files
Wildcards	

OPEN A FILE FROM THE FILE MANAGER

You can open a file directly from the File Manager. This enables you to review and make changes to the file.

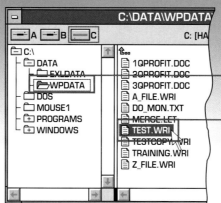

1 Move the mouse ⍟ over the directory that contains the file you want to open (example: **WPDATA**) and then press the left button.

2 Move the mouse ⍟ over the file you want to open (example: **TEST.WRI**) and then quickly press the left button twice.

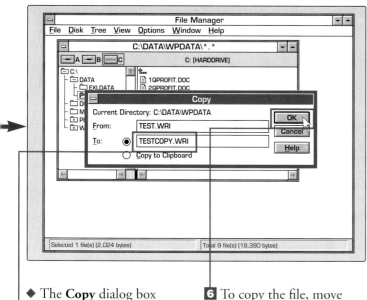

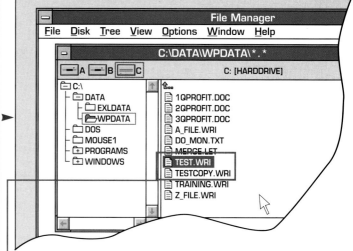

◆ The **Copy** dialog box appears.

5 Type a new name for the file (example: **TESTCOPY.WRI**).

Note: You must give the copied file a new name since each file name in a directory must be different.

6 To copy the file, move the mouse ⍟ over **OK** and then press the left button.

*Note: To cancel the copy, move the mouse ⍟ over **Cancel** and then press the left button.*

◆ Windows copies the file and gives the copy the name you specified. Both files reside in the same directory (example: **TEST.WRI** and **TESTCOPY.WRI**).

MOVE OR COPY FILES

As a precaution, copy your files to a diskette. You can then use these copies to replace any lost data if your hard drive fails or you accidentally erase a file.

Copy Files (to a Different Drive)

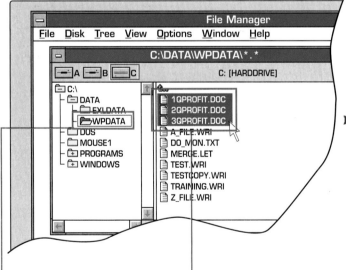

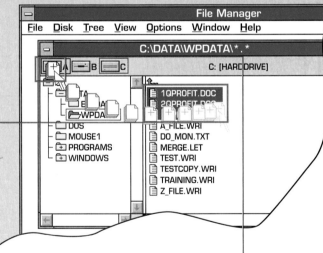

1 Move the mouse ⬚ over the directory that contains the files you want to copy (example: **WPDATA**) and then press the left button.

*Assumption: The **File Manager** is open. To open the **File Manager**, refer to page 48.*

2 Select the files you want to copy to a different drive.

Note: To select files, refer to pages 84 to 89.

3 Move the mouse ⬚ over one of the highlighted files and then press and hold down the left button.

4 Still holding down the button, move the mouse ⬚ over the drive where you want to copy the files (example: **drive A**) and then release the button.

Note: Make sure you have a formatted diskette in the drive where you want to copy the files.

INTRODUCTION TO WINDOWS

| Getting Started | Windows Basics | Help | Manage Your Applications | Manage Your Directories | **Manage Your Files** | Manage Your Diskettes | Manage Your Work |

MOVE FILES TO A DIFFERENT DRIVE

The Move command places exact copies of your files in a new location. Windows deletes the original files.

◆ Repeat steps **1** to **3** below. Then press and hold down **Alt** before dragging the files in step **4**.

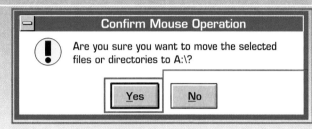

◆ The **Confirm Mouse Operation** dialog box appears.

◆ To move the files, move the mouse ⌖ over **Yes** and then press the left button.

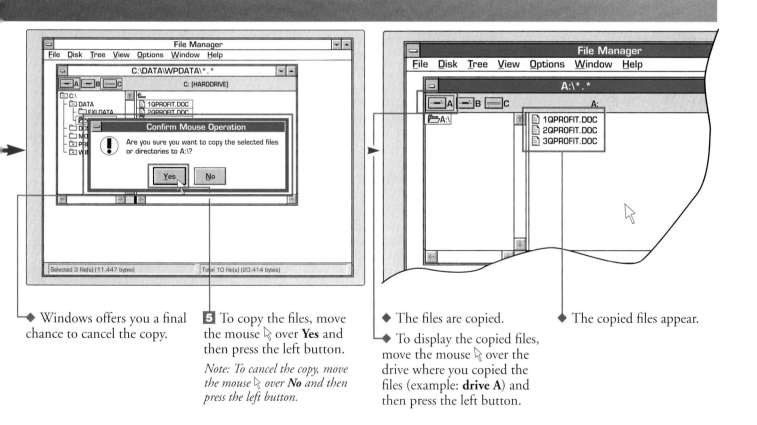

◆ Windows offers you a final chance to cancel the copy.

5 To copy the files, move the mouse ⌖ over **Yes** and then press the left button.

*Note: To cancel the copy, move the mouse ⌖ over **No** and then press the left button.*

◆ The files are copied.

◆ To display the copied files, move the mouse ⌖ over the drive where you copied the files (example: **drive A**) and then press the left button.

◆ The copied files appear.

RENAME
A FILE

You can change the name of a file stored on a disk. This enables you to give the file a name that better describes its contents.

Rename a File

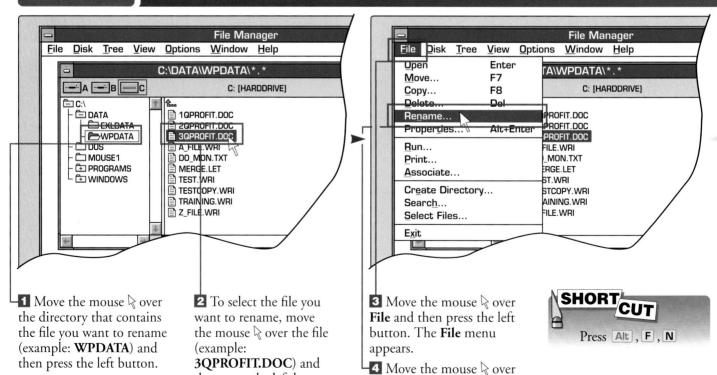

1 Move the mouse ⬚ over the directory that contains the file you want to rename (example: **WPDATA**) and then press the left button.

*Assumption: The **File Manager** is open. To open the **File Manager**, refer to page 48.*

2 To select the file you want to rename, move the mouse ⬚ over the file (example: **3QPROFIT.DOC**) and then press the left button.

3 Move the mouse ⬚ over **File** and then press the left button. The **File** menu appears.

4 Move the mouse ⬚ over **Rename** and then press the left button.

SHORT CUT

Press Alt , F , N

INTRODUCTION TO WINDOWS

| Getting Started | Windows Basics | Help | Manage Your Applications | Manage Your Directories | **Manage Your Files** | Manage Your Diskettes | Manage Your Work |

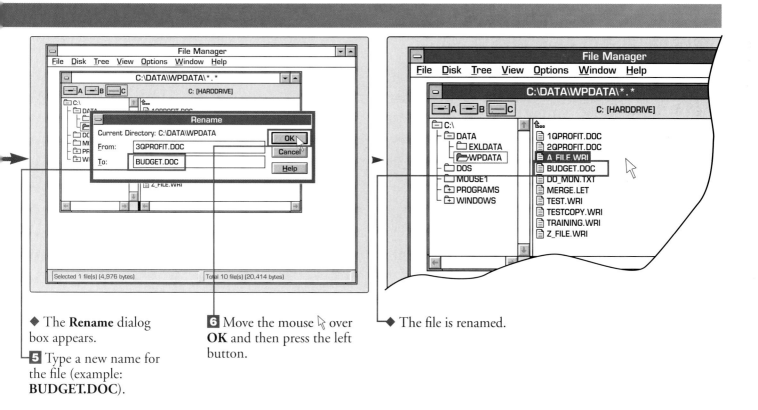

◆ The **Rename** dialog box appears.

5 Type a new name for the file (example: **BUDGET.DOC**).

6 Move the mouse ▷ over **OK** and then press the left button.

◆ The file is renamed.

97

DELETE
FILES

You can delete a file that you no longer require to make room for new files.

Delete Files

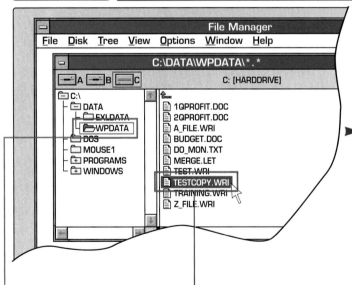

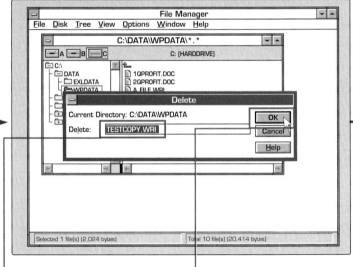

1 Move the mouse ⌖ over the directory that contains the file(s) you want to delete (example: **WPDATA**) and then press the left button.

*Assumption: The **File Manager** is open. To open the **File Manager**, refer to page 48.*

2 Select the file(s) you want to delete (example: **TESTCOPY.WRI**).

Note: To select files, refer to pages 84 to 89.

3 Press Delete and the **Delete** dialog box appears.

◆ Windows displays the name(s) of the file(s) it will delete (example: **TESTCOPY.WRI**).

4 Move the mouse ⌖ over **OK** and then press the left button.

INTRODUCTION TO WINDOWS

| Getting Started | Windows Basics | Help | Manage Your Applications | Manage Your Directories | **Manage Your Files** | Manage Your Diskettes | Manage Your Work |

◆ Make sure you do not delete files you may need in the future.

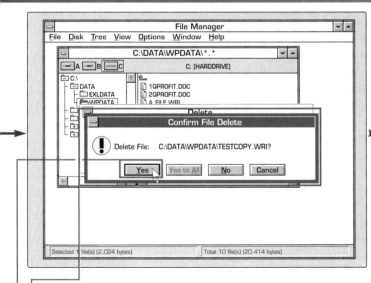

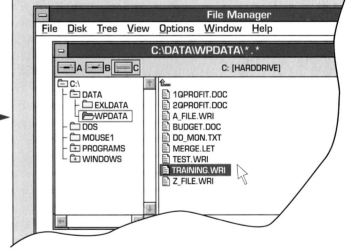

◆ Windows offers you a final chance to cancel the deletion.

5 To delete the file, move the mouse ⌖ over **Yes** and then press the left button.

Note: If you do not want to delete the file, move the mouse ⌖ over No and then press the left button.

6 If you selected more than one file in step **2**, repeat step **5** until you have deleted all the files.

or

To delete all the files at the same time, move the mouse ⌖ over **Yes to All** and then press the left button.

◆ The file is deleted.

Uses of Diskettes

You can protect the files stored on your computer by copying them to diskettes. These will serve as backup copies if your hard drive fails or you accidentally erase important files.

TRANSFER FILES TO ANOTHER COMPUTER

You can use diskettes to transfer files from one computer to another.

FREE HARD DISK SPACE

You can copy old or rarely used files to diskettes. Remove these files from your hard drive to free disk space.

INTRODUCTION TO WINDOWS

| Getting Started | Windows Basics | Help | Manage Your Applications | Manage Your Directories | Manage Your Files | **Manage Your Diskettes** | Manage Your Work |

Introduction
Format a Disk
Copy a Disk
Label a Disk

5.25 Inch Diskettes

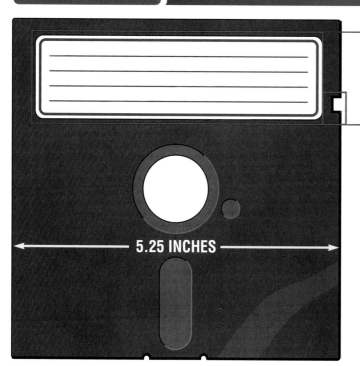

5.25 INCHES

◆ Most 5.25 inch diskettes provide you with a label to describe their contents. Use a soft-tipped felt marker to write on the label. A pen or pencil may damage the diskette.

◆ You can prevent erasing and recording information on this diskette by placing a small sticker over the "Write-Protect" notch.

Not Write-Protected

Write-Protected

INSERTING A 5.25 INCH DISKETTE

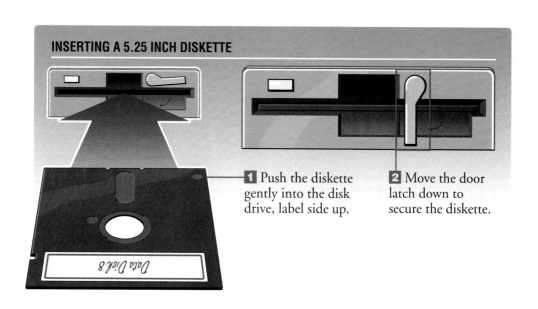

Data Disk 8

1 Push the diskette gently into the disk drive, label side up.

2 Move the door latch down to secure the diskette.

3.5 Inch Diskettes

3.5 INCHES

◆ Most 3.5 inch diskettes provide you with a label to describe their contents. Use a soft-tipped felt marker to write on the label. A pen or pencil may damage the diskette.

◆ You can prevent erasing and recording information on this diskette by moving the tab to the "Write-Protected" position.

Not Write-Protected

Write-Protected

INSERTING A 3.5 INCH DISKETTE

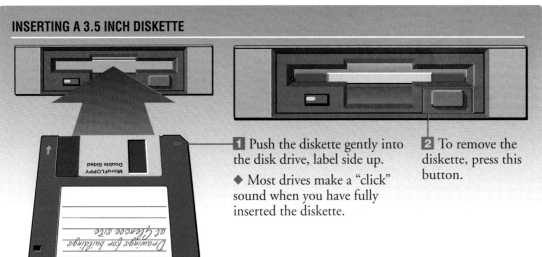

1 Push the diskette gently into the disk drive, label side up.

◆ Most drives make a "click" sound when you have fully inserted the diskette.

2 To remove the diskette, press this button.

Never insert or remove a diskette when the disk drive light is on.

INTRODUCTION TO WINDOWS

| Getting Started | Windows Basics | Help | Manage Your Applications | Manage Your Directories | Manage Your Files | **Manage Your Diskettes** | Manage Your Work |

Introduction
Format a Disk
Copy a Disk
Label a Disk

Diskette Capacity

The capacity of a diskette tells you how much information a diskette can store.

If a typed page contains 1,000 characters (approximately 1K), then a 720K diskette can store 720 pages of information.

Note: 1,000K approximately equals 1MB.

720 **PAGES**

1 **PAGE**

1K   720K

3.5 and 5.25 inch diskettes offer two types of storage capacities.

◆ A high-density diskette can store more information than a double-density diskette of the same size.

◆ High-density 3.5 inch diskettes usually display the **HD** symbol. They also have two holes at the top of the diskette. Double-density diskettes have only one hole.

Type	Capacity
Double-density	720K
High-density	1.44MB

◆ Double-density 5.25 inch diskettes are usually labeled. They also display a double ring. High-density diskettes do not display a double ring.

Type	Capacity
Double-density	360K
High-density	1.2MB

FORMAT
A DISK

You must format a diskette before storing data on it. Formatting prepares the disk for use.

Format a Disk

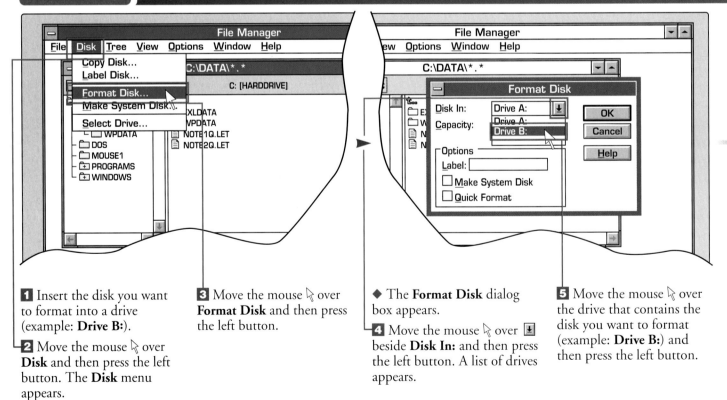

1 Insert the disk you want to format into a drive (example: **Drive B:**).

2 Move the mouse ⬚ over **Disk** and then press the left button. The **Disk** menu appears.

3 Move the mouse ⬚ over **Format Disk** and then press the left button.

◆ The **Format Disk** dialog box appears.

4 Move the mouse ⬚ over ⬇ beside **Disk In:** and then press the left button. A list of drives appears.

5 Move the mouse ⬚ over the drive that contains the disk you want to format (example: **Drive B:**) and then press the left button.

104

Getting
Started

Windows
Basics

Help

Manage
Your Applications

Manage
Your Directories

Manage
Your Files

**Manage
Your Diskettes**

Manage
Your Work

Introduction
Format a Disk
Copy a Disk
Label a Disk

◆ The Format command erases all the information on your diskette. Do not format a diskette containing information you want to keep.

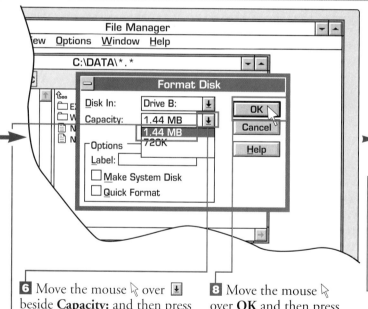

6 Move the mouse � over ⊞ beside **Capacity:** and then press the left button. A list of capacities appears.

7 Move the mouse � over the storage capacity of the disk you are about to format (example: **1.44 MB**) and then press the left button.

Note: For information on disk storage capacity, refer to page 103.

8 Move the mouse � over **OK** and then press the left button.

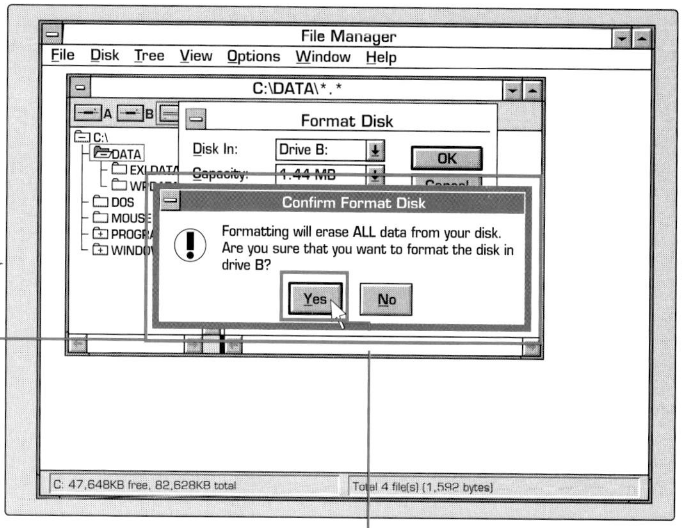

◆ This dialog box offers you a final chance to cancel the format.

*Note: To cancel the format, move the mouse � over **No** and then press the left button.*

9 To format the disk, move the mouse � over **Yes** and then press the left button.

Note: To continue, refer to the next page.

Format a Disk (continued)

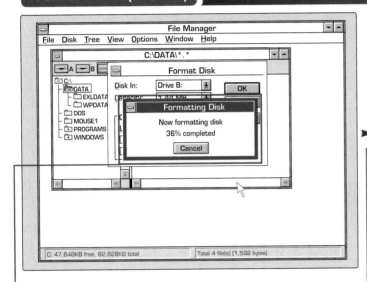

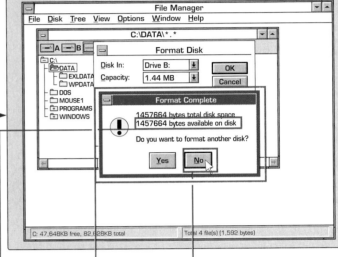

◆ A dialog box appears displaying the progress of the format.

Note: To start the format, refer to the previous page.

◆ This dialog box appears when the format is complete.

◆ The total bytes available on the disk are displayed.

10 If you do not want to format another disk, move the mouse ⌖ over **No** and then press the left button.

*Note: To format another disk, move the mouse ⌖ over **Yes** and then press the left button.*

TIP

◆ If these values are different, the diskette may have damaged areas. Your computer will not save data in these areas.

INTRODUCTION TO WINDOWS

| Getting Started | Windows Basics | Help | Manage Your Applications | Manage Your Directories | Manage Your Files | **Manage Your Diskettes** | Manage Your Work |

> *The Copy Disk command enables you to copy the entire contents of one diskette to another. The second diskette becomes an exact copy of the first one.*

Source Disk

Note: The source and destination diskettes must be the same size and capacity.

Destination Disk

Copy a Disk

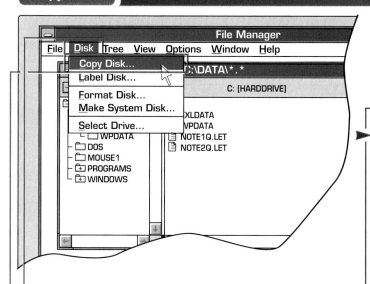

1 Move the mouse ⟍ over **Disk** and then press the left button. The **Disk** menu appears.

2 Move the mouse ⟍ over **Copy Disk** and then press the left button.

SHORT CUT
Press Alt , D , C

◆ The **Copy Disk** dialog box appears only if your computer has two disk drives (**A:** and **B:**).

◆ To change the source or destination drive, move the mouse ⟍ over an arrow ▼ and then press the left button. Move the mouse ⟍ over the drive you want to use and then press the left button.

3 Move the mouse ⟍ over **OK** and then press the left button.

Note: To continue, refer to the next page.

COPY
A DISK

When using the Copy Disk command, make sure the destination diskette does not contain information you want to keep. The Copy Disk command will permanently erase the data from the disk.

Copy a Disk (continued)

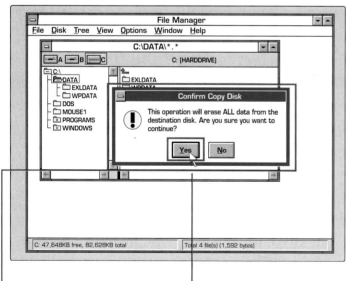

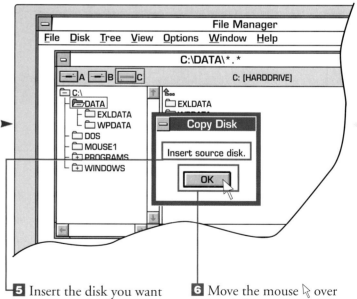

◆ This dialog box offers you a final chance to cancel the copy.

Note: To start the copy, refer to the previous page.

4 To copy the disk, move the mouse ⤢ over **Yes** and then press the left button.

*Note: To cancel the copy, move the mouse ⤢ over **No** and then press the left button.*

5 Insert the disk you want to copy into the drive you specified (example: **Drive A:**).

6 Move the mouse ⤢ over **OK** and then press the left button.

INTRODUCTION TO WINDOWS

| Getting Started | Windows Basics | Help | Manage Your Applications | Manage Your Directories | Manage Your Files | **Manage Your Diskettes** | Manage Your Work |

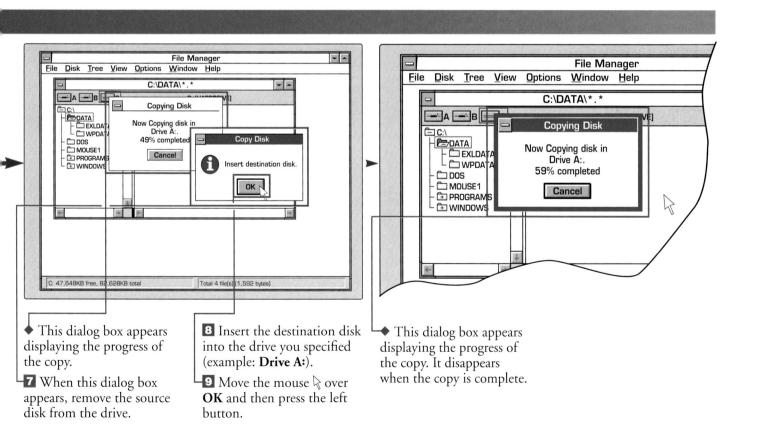

◆ This dialog box appears displaying the progress of the copy.

7 When this dialog box appears, remove the source disk from the drive.

8 Insert the destination disk into the drive you specified (example: **Drive A:**).

9 Move the mouse ⌖ over **OK** and then press the left button.

◆ This dialog box appears displaying the progress of the copy. It disappears when the copy is complete.

LABEL
A DISK

You can add or change an electronic label on a diskette. This enables you to quickly identify its contents.

Label a Disk

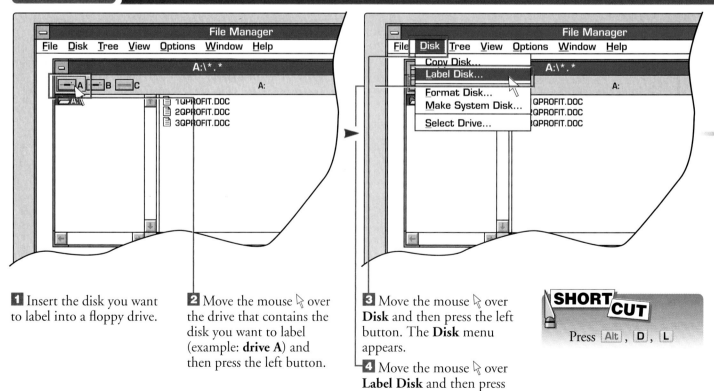

1 Insert the disk you want to label into a floppy drive.

2 Move the mouse ⃗ over the drive that contains the disk you want to label (example: **drive A**) and then press the left button.

3 Move the mouse ⃗ over **Disk** and then press the left button. The **Disk** menu appears.

4 Move the mouse ⃗ over **Label Disk** and then press the left button.

SHORTCUT

Press Alt , D , L

INTRODUCTION TO WINDOWS

| Getting Started | Windows Basics | Help | Manage Your Applications | Manage Your Directories | Manage Your Files | **Manage Your Diskettes** | Manage Your Work |

Manage Your Diskettes
Introduction
Format a Disk
Copy a Disk
Label a Disk

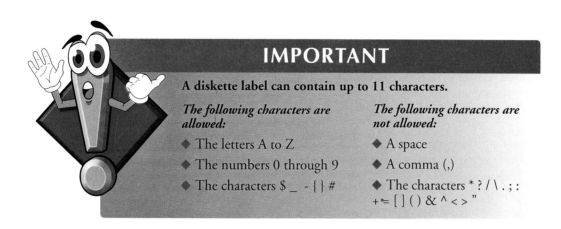

IMPORTANT

A diskette label can contain up to 11 characters.

The following characters are allowed:

◆ The letters A to Z

◆ The numbers 0 through 9

◆ The characters $ _ - { } #

The following characters are not allowed:

◆ A space

◆ A comma (,)

◆ The characters * ? / \ . ; : + = [ ] ( ) & ^ < > "

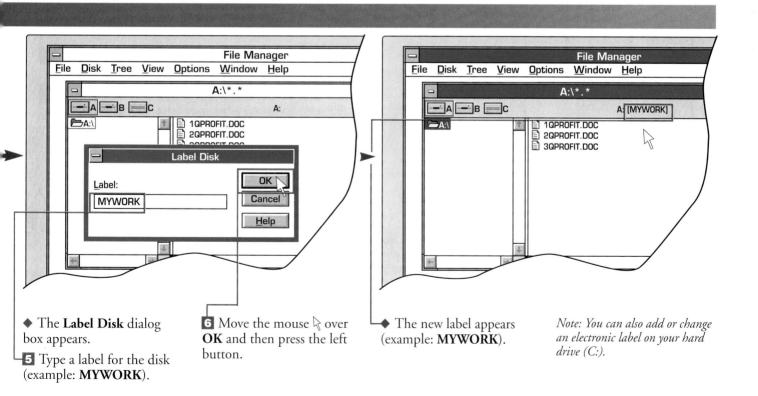

◆ The **Label Disk** dialog box appears.

5 Type a label for the disk (example: **MYWORK**).

6 Move the mouse ⇗ over **OK** and then press the left button.

◆ The new label appears (example: **MYWORK**).

Note: You can also add or change an electronic label on your hard drive (C:).

START APPLICATIONS AUTOMATICALLY

You can have one or more applications open automatically each time you start Windows. This will save you time if you always use the same applications in Windows.

Start Applications Automatically

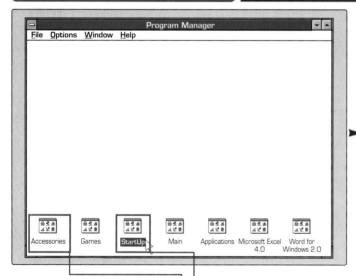

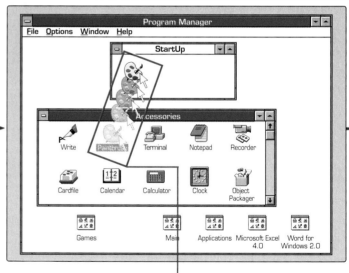

You can place an application icon in the StartUp group window. The application will then automatically open each time you start Windows.

1 Open the **StartUp** group window.

2 Open the group window that contains the application you want to start automatically (example: **Accessories**).

Note: To open a group window, move the mouse ⃕ over its icon and then quickly press the left button twice.

3 Size and move the windows as shown above.

Note: To size a window, refer to page 14. To move a window, refer to page 12.

4 To copy an application icon to the **StartUp** window, press and hold down Ctrl .

5 Still holding down Ctrl , move the mouse ⃕ over the application icon (example: **Paintbrush**) and then press and hold down the left button as you drag the icon to the **StartUp** window.

INTRODUCTION TO WINDOWS

| Getting Started | Windows Basics | Help | Manage Your Applications | Manage Your Directories | Manage Your Files | Manage Your Diskettes | **Manage Your Work** |

Start Applications Automatically
Create a Group Window
Copy Files to a Group Window

DELETE AN APPLICATION ICON

1 Move the mouse ⌖ over the application icon you want to delete (example: **Paintbrush**) and then press the left button.

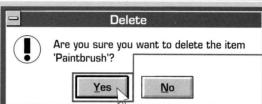

2 Press Delete and the **Delete** dialog box appears.

3 To delete the application icon, move the mouse ⌖ over **Yes** and then press the left button.

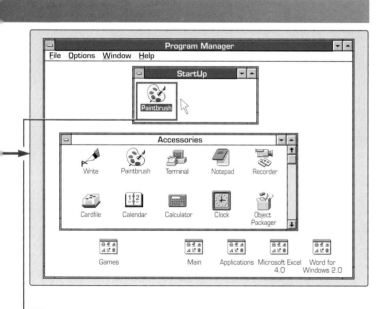

6 Release the button and then release Ctrl . A copy of the application icon appears in the **StartUp** group window.

Note: You can place more than one application icon in the **StartUp** *group window. All applications in this window will automatically open each time you start Windows.*

The next time you start Windows, all applications in the StartUp group window will automatically open (example: Paintbrush).

CREATE A GROUP WINDOW

You can create a group window to store programs and files you frequently use. This will save you both time and effort by keeping all the information you need in one location.

Create a Group Window

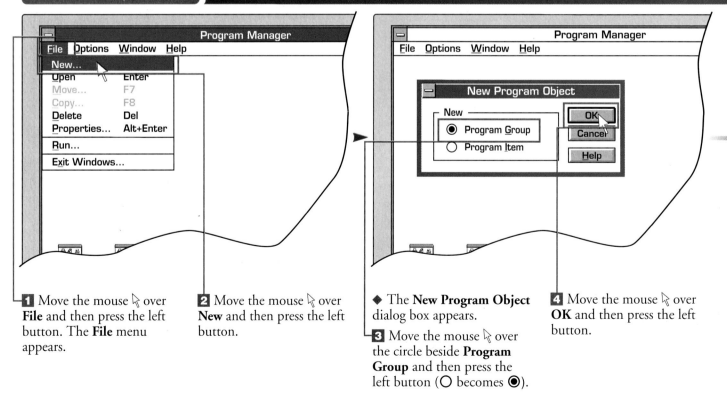

1 Move the mouse ⬚ over **File** and then press the left button. The **File** menu appears.

2 Move the mouse ⬚ over **New** and then press the left button.

◆ The **New Program Object** dialog box appears.

3 Move the mouse ⬚ over the circle beside **Program Group** and then press the left button (○ becomes ⊙).

4 Move the mouse ⬚ over **OK** and then press the left button.

INTRODUCTION TO WINDOWS

| Getting Started | Windows Basics | Help | Manage Your Applications | Manage Your Directories | Manage Your Files | Manage Your Diskettes | **Manage Your Work** |

DELETE A GROUP WINDOW

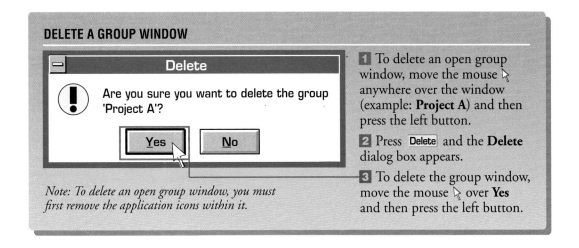

Delete

Are you sure you want to delete the group 'Project A'?

Yes   No

Note: To delete an open group window, you must first remove the application icons within it.

1 To delete an open group window, move the mouse ⌖ anywhere over the window (example: **Project A**) and then press the left button.

2 Press `Delete` and the **Delete** dialog box appears.

3 To delete the group window, move the mouse ⌖ over **Yes** and then press the left button.

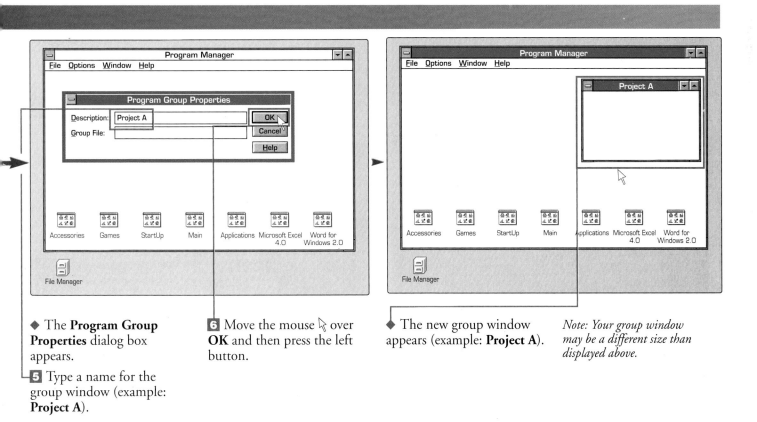

◆ The **Program Group Properties** dialog box appears.

5 Type a name for the group window (example: **Project A**).

6 Move the mouse ⌖ over **OK** and then press the left button.

◆ The new group window appears (example: **Project A**).

Note: Your group window may be a different size than displayed above.

COPY FILES TO A GROUP WINDOW

You can copy files you frequently use to a group window. This can save you time by keeping all your important information in one location.

Copy Files to a Group Window

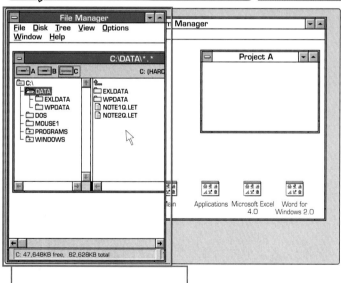

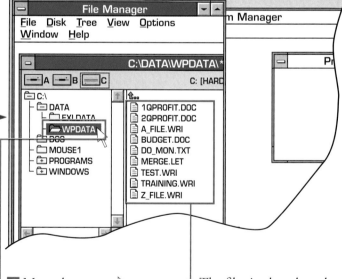

1 Open the **File Manager**.

*Note: To open the **File Manager**, refer to page 48.*

2 Size and move the **File Manager** window as shown above.

Note: To size a window, refer to page 14. To move a window, refer to page 12.

3 Move the mouse ⬚ over the directory that contains the files you want to copy (example: **WPDATA**) and then press the left button.

◆ The files in the selected directory appear.

INTRODUCTION TO WINDOWS

| Getting Started | Windows Basics | Help | Manage Your Applications | Manage Your Directories | Manage Your Files | Manage Your Diskettes | **Manage Your Work** |

Start Applications Automatically
Create a Group Window
Copy Files to a Group Window

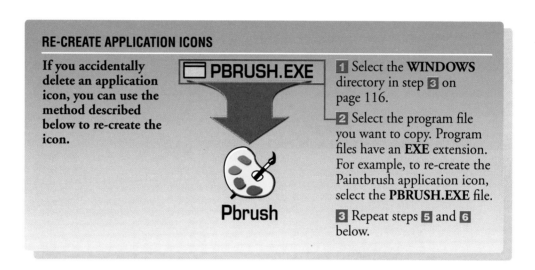

RE-CREATE APPLICATION ICONS

If you accidentally delete an application icon, you can use the method described below to re-create the icon.

PBRUSH.EXE

Pbrush

1 Select the **WINDOWS** directory in step **3** on page 116.

2 Select the program file you want to copy. Program files have an **EXE** extension. For example, to re-create the Paintbrush application icon, select the **PBRUSH.EXE** file.

3 Repeat steps **5** and **6** below.

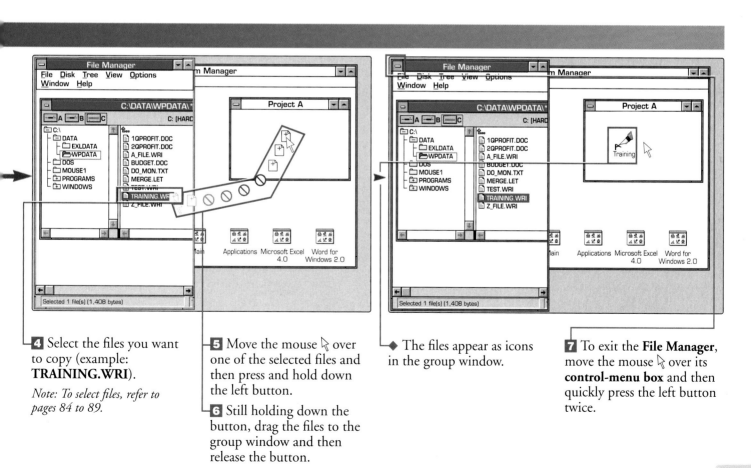

4 Select the files you want to copy (example: **TRAINING.WRI**).

Note: To select files, refer to pages 84 to 89.

5 Move the mouse ⭧ over one of the selected files and then press and hold down the left button.

6 Still holding down the button, drag the files to the group window and then release the button.

◆ The files appear as icons in the group window.

7 To exit the **File Manager**, move the mouse ⭧ over its **control-menu box** and then quickly press the left button twice.

117

The Write program is a simple word processor that enables you to write letters, memos and reports. You can take advantage of the editing and formatting features to produce professional documents.

Start Write

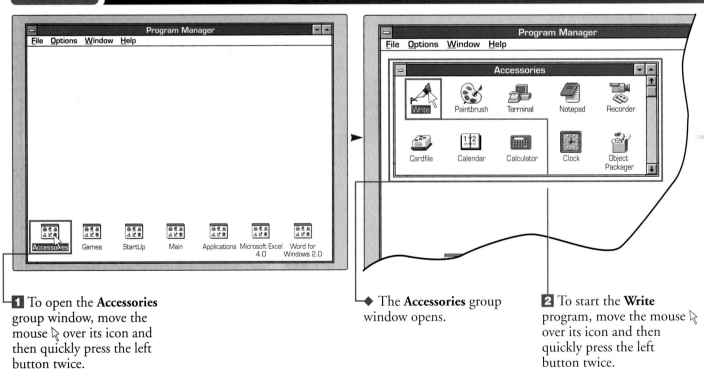

1 To open the **Accessories** group window, move the mouse over its icon and then quickly press the left button twice.

◆ The **Accessories** group window opens.

2 To start the **Write** program, move the mouse over its icon and then quickly press the left button twice.

| Accessories | Print | Control Panel | Run DOS in Windows | Sharing Data | Improve Windows Performance |

WRITE

Start Write	Exit Write
Enter Text	Open a Document
Move Within Write	Edit Text
Select Text	Justify Text
Change Fonts	Tabs
Change Margins	Move Text
Save a Document	

CARDFILE

PAINTBRUSH

CALENDAR

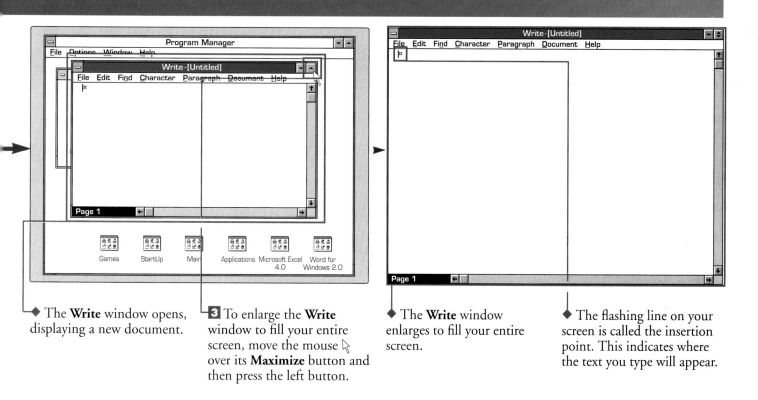

◆ The **Write** window opens, displaying a new document.

3 To enlarge the **Write** window to fill your entire screen, move the mouse over its **Maximize** button and then press the left button.

◆ The **Write** window enlarges to fill your entire screen.

◆ The flashing line on your screen is called the insertion point. This indicates where the text you type will appear.

When typing text in your document, you do not need to press `Enter` *at the end of a line. Write automatically moves the text to the next line. This is called "word wrapping."*

When using a word processor to type a letter, the text au...

When using a word processor to type a letter, the text automatically wraps to the next line as you type.

Enter Text

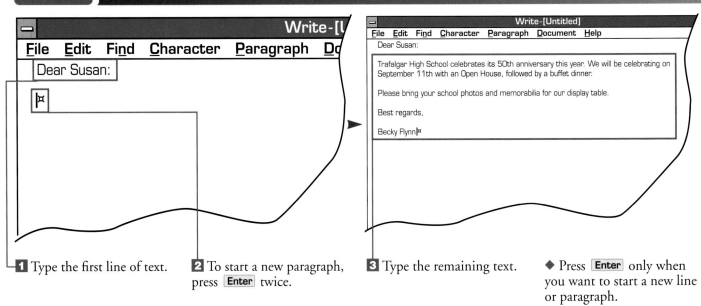

1 Type the first line of text.

2 To start a new paragraph, press `Enter` twice.

3 Type the remaining text.

◆ Press `Enter` only when you want to start a new line or paragraph.

Accessories		Print	Control Panel	Run DOS in Windows	Sharing Data	Improve Windows Performance

WRITE	Start Write	Exit Write
CARDFILE	**Enter Text**	Open a Document
	Move Within Write	Edit Text
PAINTBRUSH	Select Text	Justify Text
	Change Fonts	Tabs
CALENDAR	Change Margins	Move Text
	Save a Document	

MOVE WITHIN WRITE (USING THE KEYBOARD)

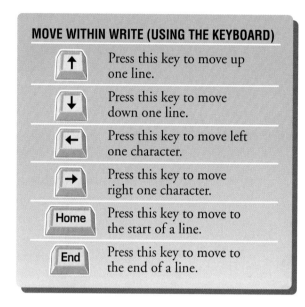

Press this key to move up one line.

Press this key to move down one line.

Press this key to move left one character.

Press this key to move right one character.

Home Press this key to move to the start of a line.

End Press this key to move to the end of a line.

Move Within Write (Using the Mouse)

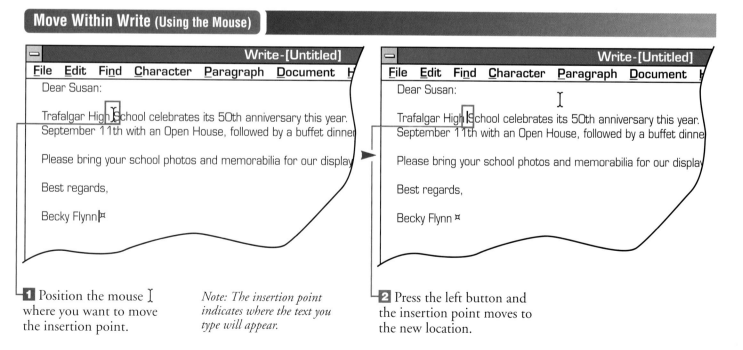

1 Position the mouse I where you want to move the insertion point.

Note: The insertion point indicates where the text you type will appear.

2 Press the left button and the insertion point moves to the new location.

SELECT TEXT

To perform a command on a section of text, you must first select the text. This highlights (isolates) the text so Write knows to work with only those characters.

Select a Word

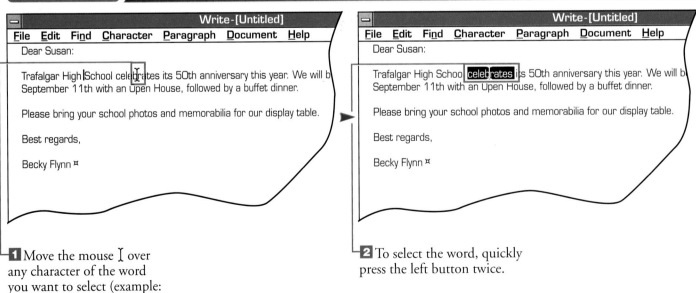

1 Move the mouse I over any character of the word you want to select (example: **celebrates**).

2 To select the word, quickly press the left button twice.

Accessories	Print	Control Panel	Run DOS in Windows	Sharing Data	Improve Windows Performance

WRITE	Start Write	Exit Write
CARDFILE	Enter Text	Open a Document
	Move Within Write	Edit Text
PAINTBRUSH	**Select Text**	Justify Text
	Change Fonts	Tabs
CALENDAR	Change Margins	Move Text
	Save a Document	

SELECT A SENTENCE

1 Press and hold down Ctrl.

2 Still holding down Ctrl, move the mouse I anywhere over the sentence you want to select and then press the left button.

SELECT THE ENTIRE DOCUMENT

1 Press and hold down Ctrl.

2 Still holding down Ctrl, move the mouse I to the left of the text in your document and I changes to ↗. Then press the left button.

TIP

◆ To cancel a text selection, press the left button.

Select any Amount of Text

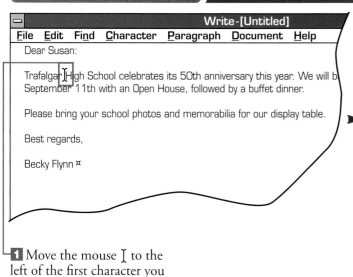

Write-[Untitled]

File   Edit   Find   Character   Paragraph   Document   Help

Dear Susan:

Trafalgar High School celebrates its 50th anniversary this year. We will b
September 11th with an Open House, followed by a buffet dinner.

Please bring your school photos and memorabilia for our display table.

Best regards,

Becky Flynn ¤

Write-[Untitled]

File   Edit   Find   Character   Paragraph   Document   Help

Dear Susan:

Trafalgar High School celebrates its 50th anniversary this year. We will b
September 11th with an Open House, followed by a buffet dinner.

Please bring your school photos and memorabilia for our display table.

Best regards,

Becky Flynn ¤

1 Move the mouse I to the left of the first character you want to select.

2 To select the text, press and hold down the left button and then drag the mouse I until you highlight the text.

3 Release the button.

CHANGE FONTS

You can emphasize information in your document by using different fonts.

FONT

You can change the design of the characters in your document. Some examples are:

Arial

Courier

Letter Gothic

Times New Roman

FONT STYLE

You can change the style of the characters in your document. Some examples are:

Regular

Italic

Bold

Change Fonts

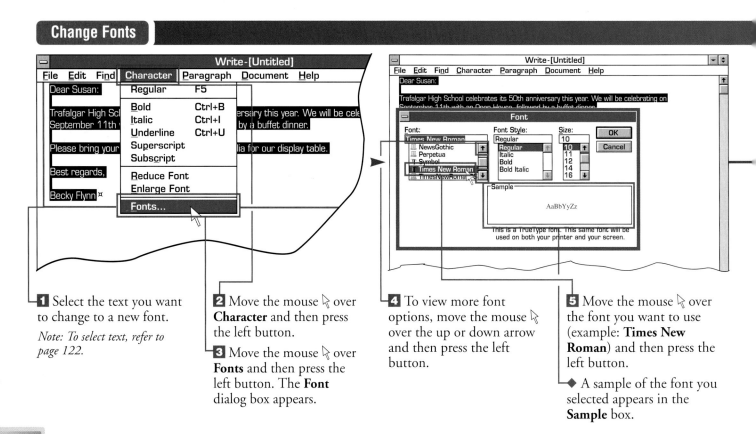

1 Select the text you want to change to a new font.

Note: To select text, refer to page 122.

2 Move the mouse ⇖ over **Character** and then press the left button.

3 Move the mouse ⇖ over **Fonts** and then press the left button. The **Font** dialog box appears.

4 To view more font options, move the mouse ⇖ over the up or down arrow and then press the left button.

5 Move the mouse ⇖ over the font you want to use (example: **Times New Roman**) and then press the left button.

◆ A sample of the font you selected appears in the **Sample** box.

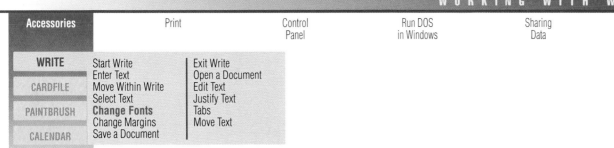

| Accessories | Print | Control Panel | Run DOS in Windows | Sharing Data | Improve Windows Performance |

WRITE	Start Write	Exit Write
CARDFILE	Enter Text	Open a Document
	Move Within Write	Edit Text
PAINTBRUSH	Select Text	Justify Text
	Change Fonts	Tabs
CALENDAR	Change Margins	Move Text
	Save a Document	

SIZE

You can change the size of the characters in your document. Some examples are:

8

12

16

20

24

Note: Write measures size in points. There are approximately 72 points per inch.

TIP For greater font selection, you can purchase fonts and install them yourself. For information on installing fonts, refer to page 190.

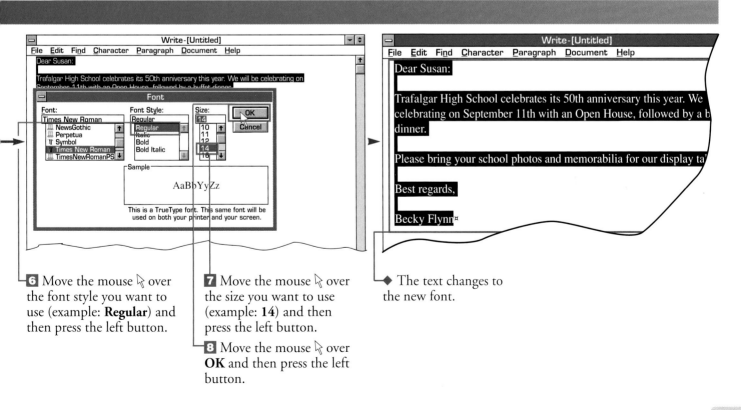

6 Move the mouse ▷ over the font style you want to use (example: **Regular**) and then press the left button.

7 Move the mouse ▷ over the size you want to use (example: **14**) and then press the left button.

8 Move the mouse ▷ over **OK** and then press the left button.

◆ The text changes to the new font.

CHANGE MARGINS

A margin is the amount of space between the text and the edges of your paper.

You can shorten or lengthen the size of your document by changing the margins.

Change Margins

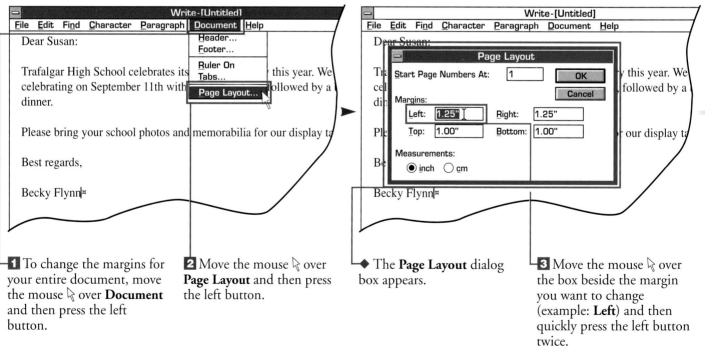

1 To change the margins for your entire document, move the mouse ⓀǏ over **Document** and then press the left button.

2 Move the mouse ⓀǏ over **Page Layout** and then press the left button.

◆ The **Page Layout** dialog box appears.

3 Move the mouse ⓀǏ over the box beside the margin you want to change (example: **Left**) and then quickly press the left button twice.

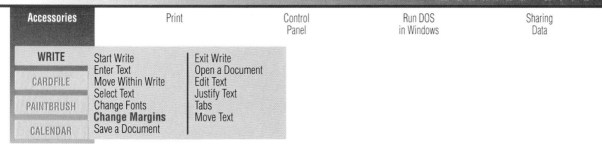

| Accessories | Print | Control Panel | Run DOS in Windows | Sharing Data | Improve Windows Performance |

WRITE
CARDFILE
PAINTBRUSH
CALENDAR

Start Write
Enter Text
Move Within Write
Select Text
Change Fonts
Change Margins
Save a Document

Exit Write
Open a Document
Edit Text
Justify Text
Tabs
Move Text

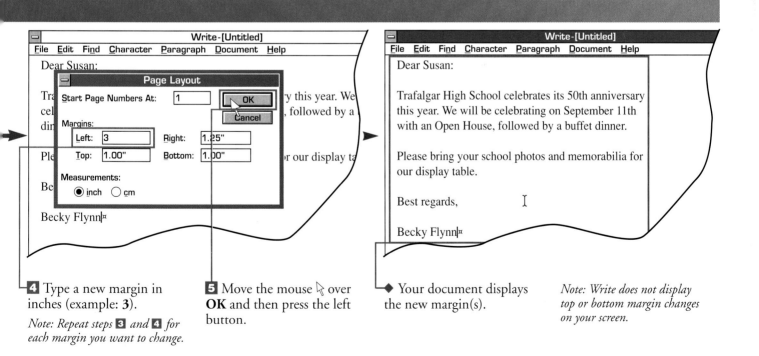

4 Type a new margin in inches (example: **3**).

*Note: Repeat steps **3** and **4** for each margin you want to change.*

5 Move the mouse ⫸ over **OK** and then press the left button.

◆ Your document displays the new margin(s).

Note: Write does not display top or bottom margin changes on your screen.

SAVE A DOCUMENT

EXIT WRITE

When you finish working on your document, save it before starting something else or exiting Write. This permanently stores your document for future use.

Save a Document

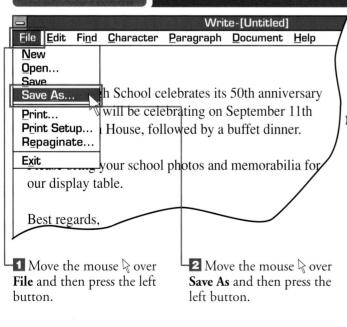

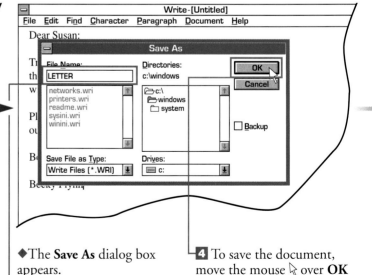

◆ The **Save As** dialog box appears.

1 Move the mouse ⟨ over **File** and then press the left button.

2 Move the mouse ⟨ over **Save As** and then press the left button.

3 Type a name for your document (example: **LETTER**).

4 To save the document, move the mouse ⟨ over **OK** and then press the left button.

| Accessories | Print | Control Panel | Run DOS in Windows | Sharing Data | Improve Windows Performance |

WRITE	Start Write	**Exit Write**
CARDFILE	Enter Text	Open a Document
	Move Within Write	Edit Text
PAINTBRUSH	Select Text	Justify Text
	Change Fonts	Tabs
CALENDAR	Change Margins	Move Text
	Save a Document	

Exiting Write will return you to the Program Manager.

Exit Write

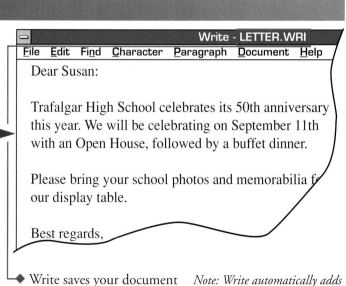

Write - LETTER.WRI

File Edit Find Character Paragraph Document Help

Dear Susan:

Trafalgar High School celebrates its 50th anniversary
this year. We will be celebrating on September 11th
with an Open House, followed by a buffet dinner.

Please bring your school photos and memorabilia f
our display table.

Best regards,

◆ Write saves your document
and displays the name at the
top of your screen.

*Note: Write automatically adds
the extension **WRI** to the file
name.*

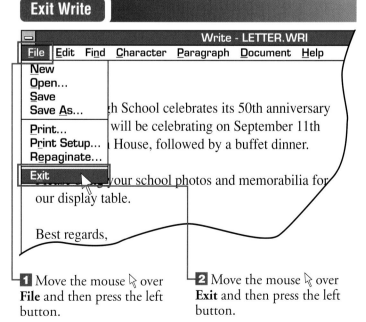

Write - LETTER.WRI

File Edit Find Character Paragraph Document Help

New
Open...
Save
Save As...

Print...
Print Setup...
Repaginate...

Exit

gh School celebrates its 50th anniversary
will be celebrating on September 11th
House, followed by a buffet dinner.

your school photos and memorabilia for
our display table.

Best regards,

1 Move the mouse over
File and then press the left
button.

2 Move the mouse over
Exit and then press the left
button.

*Note: To restart **Write**, refer to
page 118.*

OPEN A DOCUMENT

> *You can open a saved document and display it on your screen. This enables you to make changes to the document.*

Open a Document

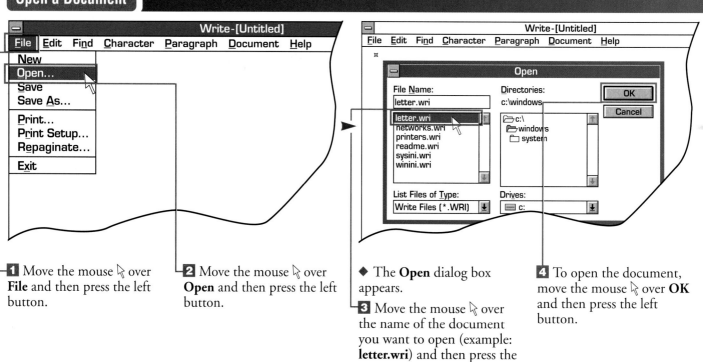

1 Move the mouse ⌖ over **File** and then press the left button.

2 Move the mouse ⌖ over **Open** and then press the left button.

◆ The **Open** dialog box appears.

3 Move the mouse ⌖ over the name of the document you want to open (example: **letter.wri**) and then press the left button.

4 To open the document, move the mouse ⌖ over **OK** and then press the left button.

Accessories	Print	Control Panel	Run DOS in Windows	Sharing Data	Improve Windows Performance

WRITE

CARDFILE

PAINTBRUSH

CALENDAR

Start Write	Exit Write
Enter Text	**Open a Document**
Move Within Write	Edit Text
Select Text	Justify Text
Change Fonts	Tabs
Change Margins	Move Text
Save a Document	

TIP

You can print your document to produce a paper copy.

Note: For information on printing a document, refer to page 166.

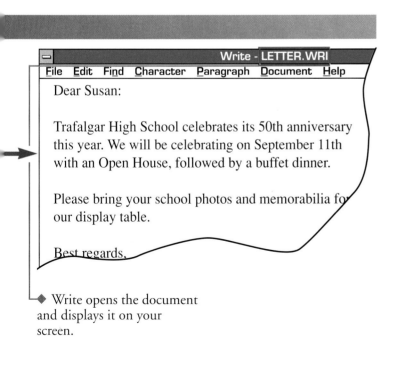

Write - LETTER.WRI

File Edit Find Character Paragraph Document Help

Dear Susan:

Trafalgar High School celebrates its 50th anniversary this year. We will be celebrating on September 11th with an Open House, followed by a buffet dinner.

Please bring your school photos and memorabilia for our display table.

Best regards,

◆ Write opens the document and displays it on your screen.

START A NEW DOCUMENT

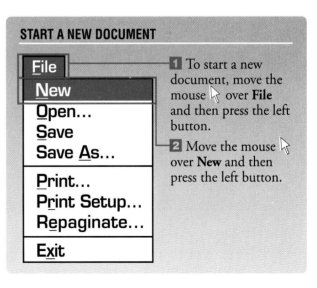

File

New
Open...
Save
Save As...

Print...
Print Setup...
Repaginate...

Exit

1 To start a new document, move the mouse over **File** and then press the left button.

2 Move the mouse over **New** and then press the left button.

EDIT TEXT

You can add and delete text from your document without having to retype a page or use correction fluid.

Insert Text

Write - LETTER.WRI

File   Edit   Find   Character   Paragraph   Document   Help

Dear Susan:

Trafalgar High School celebrates its 50th anniversary this year. We will be celebrating on September 11th with an Open House, followed by a buffet dinner.

Please bring your school photos and memorabilia for our display table.

Best regards,

Write - LETTER.WRI

File   Edit   Find   Character   Paragraph   Document   Help

Dear Susan:

Trafalgar High School celebrates its 50th anniversary this year. We will be celebrating on September 11th with an Open House, followed by a scrumptious buffet dinner.

Please bring your school photos and memorabilia for our display table.

---

1 Move the mouse I where you want to insert the new text and then press the left button.

2 Type the text you want to insert (example: **scrumptious**).

3 To insert a blank space, press the Spacebar.

Note: The words to the right of the inserted text are pushed forward.

Accessories	Print	Control Panel	Run DOS in Windows	Sharing Data	Improve Windows Performance

WRITE	Start Write	Exit Write
	Enter Text	Open a Document
CARDFILE	Move Within Write	**Edit Text**
	Select Text	Justify Text
PAINTBRUSH	Change Fonts	Tabs
	Change Margins	Move Text
CALENDAR	Save a Document	

DELETE A CHARACTER

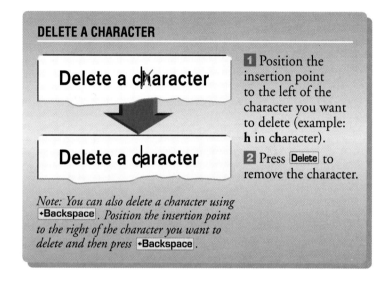

1 Position the insertion point to the left of the character you want to delete (example: **h** in character).

2 Press Delete to remove the character.

Note: You can also delete a character using **◆Backspace**. *Position the insertion point to the right of the character you want to delete and then press* **◆Backspace**.

Delete Text

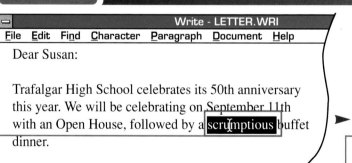

1 Select the text you want to delete (example: **scrumptious**).

Note: To select text, refer to page 122.

2 Press Delete to remove the text.

133

JUSTIFY TEXT

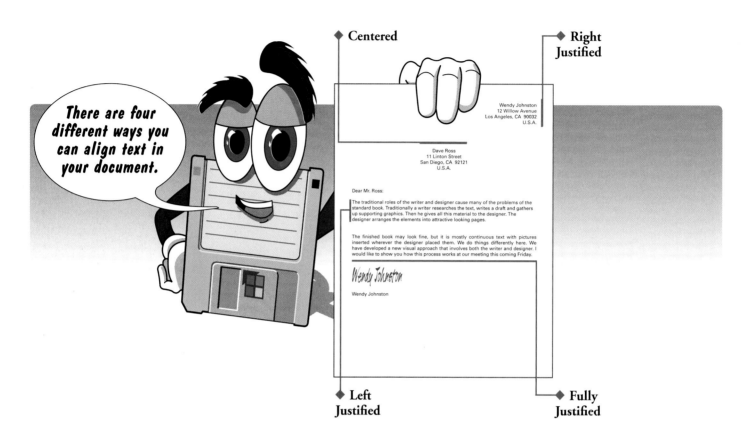

Centered

Right Justified

Left Justified

Fully Justified

There are four different ways you can align text in your document.

Justify Text

The Ruler offers these alignment options:

 This icon will left justify a paragraph.

This icon will center a paragraph.

This icon will right justify a paragraph.

This icon will fully justify a paragraph.

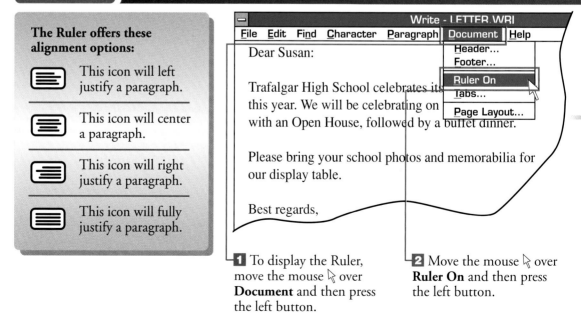

Write - LETTER.WRI

File Edit Find Character Paragraph Document Help

Dear Susan:

Trafalgar High School celebrates its
this year. We will be celebrating on
with an Open House, followed by a buffet dinner.

Please bring your school photos and memorabilia for
our display table.

Best regards,

Header...
Footer...
Ruler On
Tabs...
Page Layout...

1 To display the Ruler, move the mouse ⌖ over **Document** and then press the left button.

2 Move the mouse ⌖ over **Ruler On** and then press the left button.

| Accessories | Print | Control Panel | Run DOS in Windows | Sharing Data | Improve Windows Performance |

WRITE	Start Write	Exit Write
CARDFILE	Enter Text	Open a Document
	Move Within Write	Edit Text
	Select Text	**Justify Text**
PAINTBRUSH	Change Fonts	Tabs
	Change Margins	Move Text
CALENDAR	Save a Document	

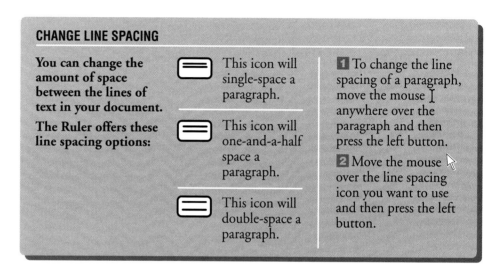

CHANGE LINE SPACING

You can change the amount of space between the lines of text in your document.

The Ruler offers these line spacing options:

This icon will single-space a paragraph.

This icon will one-and-a-half space a paragraph.

This icon will double-space a paragraph.

1 To change the line spacing of a paragraph, move the mouse I anywhere over the paragraph and then press the left button.

2 Move the mouse over the line spacing icon you want to use and then press the left button.

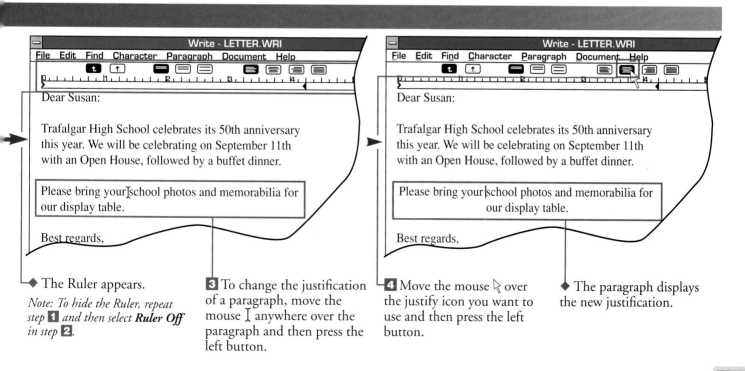

◆ The Ruler appears.

*Note: To hide the Ruler, repeat step **1** and then select **Ruler Off** in step **2**.*

3 To change the justification of a paragraph, move the mouse I anywhere over the paragraph and then press the left button.

4 Move the mouse over the justify icon you want to use and then press the left button.

◆ The paragraph displays the new justification.

TABS

You can use tabs to line up columns of information or indent a line of text.

Write offers two types of tabs:

Left Tab		Decimal Tab
Jim	Devries	$50.00
David	Johnston	$110.00
Richard	Morton	$9.00
Betty	Wu	$65.00

Add a Tab

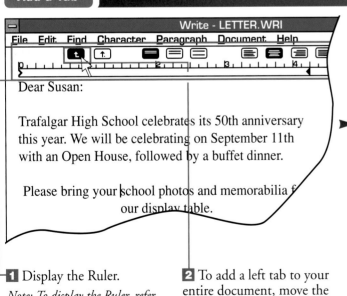

1 Display the Ruler.

Note: To display the Ruler, refer to page 134.

2 To add a left tab to your entire document, move the mouse ⬚ over [⬚] and then press the left button.

Note: To add a decimal tab, move the mouse ⬚ over [⬚] and then press the left button.

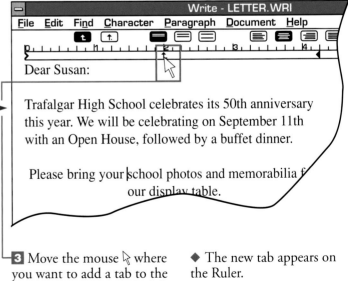

3 Move the mouse ⬚ where you want to add a tab to the Ruler and then press the left button.

◆ The new tab appears on the Ruler.

| Accessories | Print | Control Panel | Run DOS in Windows | Sharing Data | Improve Windows Performance |

WRITE	Start Write	Exit Write
CARDFILE	Enter Text	Open a Document
	Move Within Write	Edit Text
	Select Text	Justify Text
PAINTBRUSH	Change Fonts	**Tabs**
	Change Margins	Move Text
CALENDAR	Save a Document	

DELETE A TAB

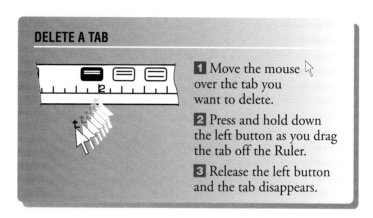

1 Move the mouse over the tab you want to delete.

2 Press and hold down the left button as you drag the tab off the Ruler.

3 Release the left button and the tab disappears.

Using Tabs

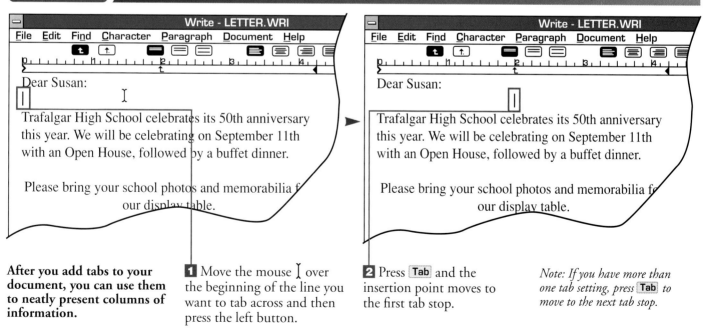

After you add tabs to your document, you can use them to neatly present columns of information.

1 Move the mouse I over the beginning of the line you want to tab across and then press the left button.

2 Press `Tab` and the insertion point moves to the first tab stop.

Note: If you have more than one tab setting, press `Tab` to move to the next tab stop.

MOVE TEXT

You can move text from one location in your document to another. Write cuts the text and pastes it in a new location. The original text disappears.

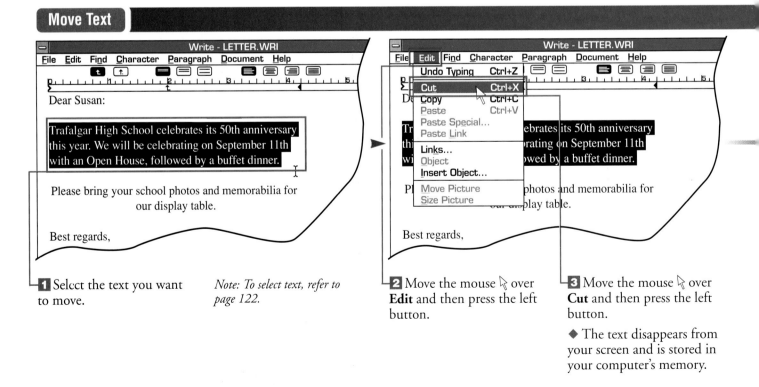

Move Text

1 Select the text you want to move.

Note: To select text, refer to page 122.

2 Move the mouse ⍾ over **Edit** and then press the left button.

3 Move the mouse ⍾ over **Cut** and then press the left button.

◆ The text disappears from your screen and is stored in your computer's memory.

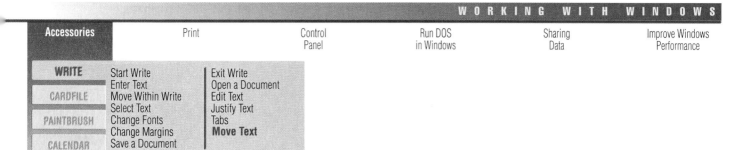

| Accessories | Print | Control Panel | Run DOS in Windows | Sharing Data | Improve Windows Performance |

WRITE   Start Write   Exit Write
CARDFILE   Enter Text   Open a Document
           Move Within Write   Edit Text
PAINTBRUSH   Select Text   Justify Text
         Change Fonts   Tabs
CALENDAR   Change Margins   **Move Text**
         Save a Document

COPY TEXT

You can copy text from one location in your document to another. Write copies the text and pastes the copy in a new location. The original text remains in its place.

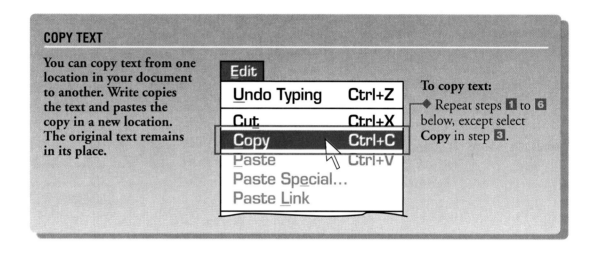

To copy text:

◆ Repeat steps **1** to **6** below, except select **Copy** in step **3**.

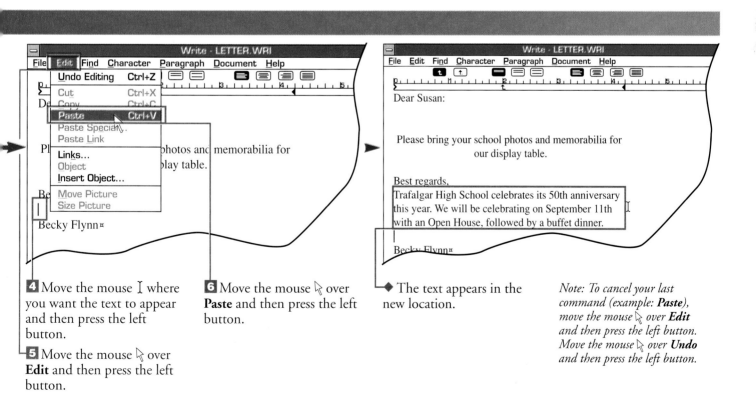

4 Move the mouse I where you want the text to appear and then press the left button.

5 Move the mouse ⊳ over **Edit** and then press the left button.

6 Move the mouse ⊳ over **Paste** and then press the left button.

◆ The text appears in the new location.

*Note: To cancel your last command (example: **Paste**), move the mouse ⊳ over **Edit** and then press the left button. Move the mouse ⊳ over **Undo** and then press the left button.*

START CARDFILE

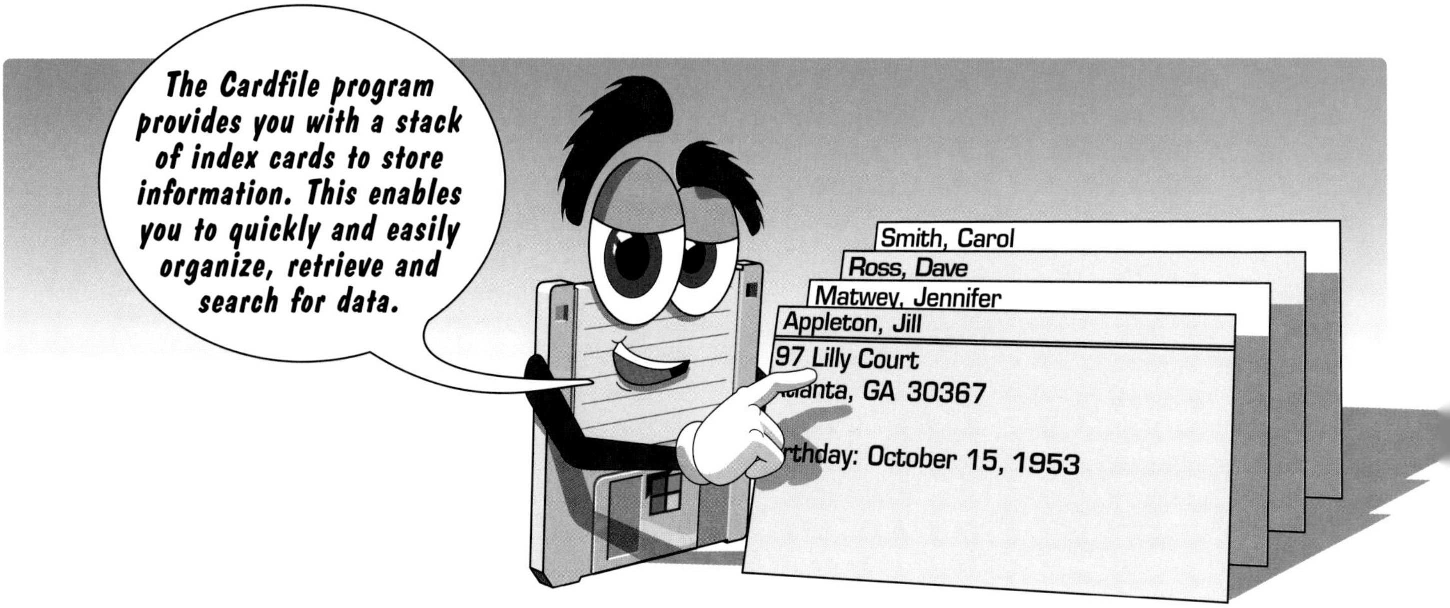
The Cardfile program provides you with a stack of index cards to store information. This enables you to quickly and easily organize, retrieve and search for data.
Smith, Carol
Ross, Dave
Matwey, Jennifer
Appleton, Jill
97 Lilly Court
GA 30367
October 15, 1953

Start Cardfile

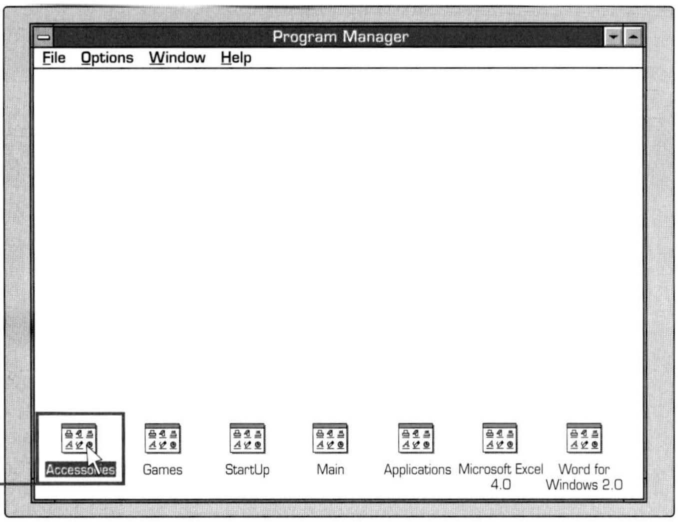
Program Manager
File Options Window Help
Accessories
Games
StartUp
Main
Applications
Microsoft Excel 4.0
Word for Windows 2.0

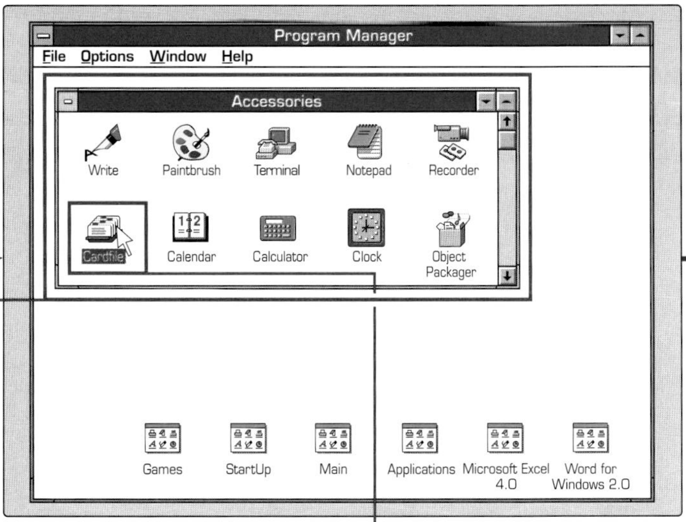
Program Manager
File Options Window Help
Accessories
Write
Paintbrush
Terminal
Notepad
Recorder
Cardfile
Calendar
Calculator
Clock
Object Packager
Games
StartUp
Main
Applications
Microsoft Excel 4.0
Word for Windows 2.0

1 To open the **Accessories** group window, move the mouse ↖ over its icon and then quickly press the left button twice.

◆ The **Accessories** group window opens.

2 To start the **Cardfile** program, move the mouse ↖ over its icon and then quickly press the left button twice.

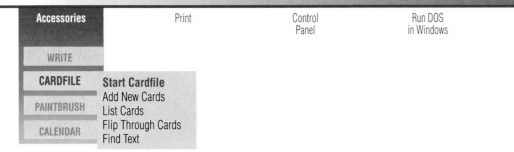

Accessories

WRITE

CARDFILE

PAINTBRUSH

CALENDAR

Print

Control
Panel

Run DOS
in Windows

Sharing
Data

Improve Windows
Performance

Start Cardfile
Add New Cards
List Cards
Flip Through Cards
Find Text

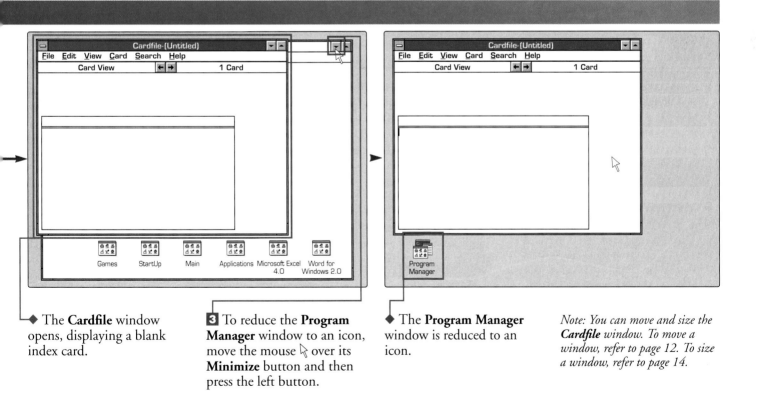

◆ The **Cardfile** window opens, displaying a blank index card.

3 To reduce the **Program Manager** window to an icon, move the mouse ⬚ over its **Minimize** button and then press the left button.

◆ The **Program Manager** window is reduced to an icon.

Note: You can move and size the ***Cardfile*** *window. To move a window, refer to page 12. To size a window, refer to page 14.*

ADD NEW CARDS

You can easily add new cards to the Cardfile. Each card has an index line that distinguishes it from other cards.
Matwey, Jennifer
57 Devon Street
San Diego, CA 92121
Smith, Caro
Ross, Dave
Appleton, Jill
97 Lilly Court
Atlanta, GA 30367
Birthday: October 15, 1953

◆ Each card has an index line.

◆ Each card can contain eleven lines of text.

Add New Cards

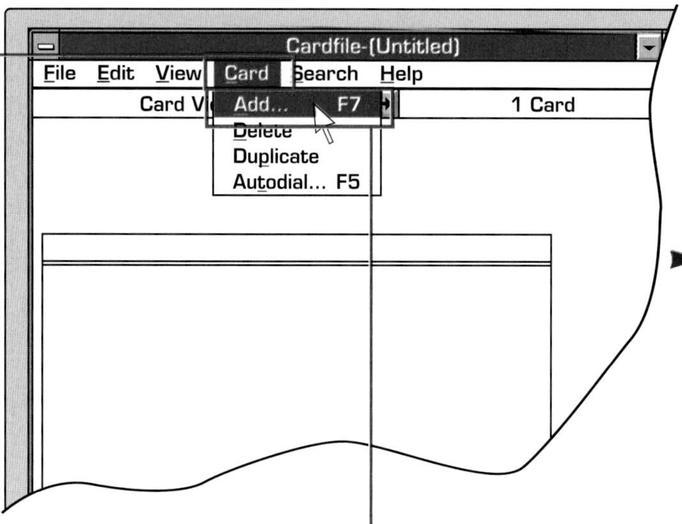

Cardfile-(Untitled)
File Edit View Card Search Help
Add... F7
Delete
Duplicate
Autodial... F5
1 Card

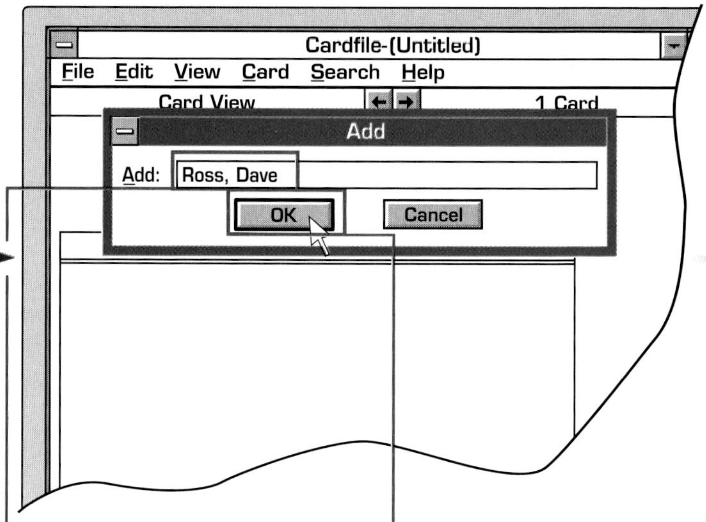

Cardfile-(Untitled)
File Edit View Card Search Help
Card View
1 Card
Add
Add: Ross, Dave
OK
Cancel

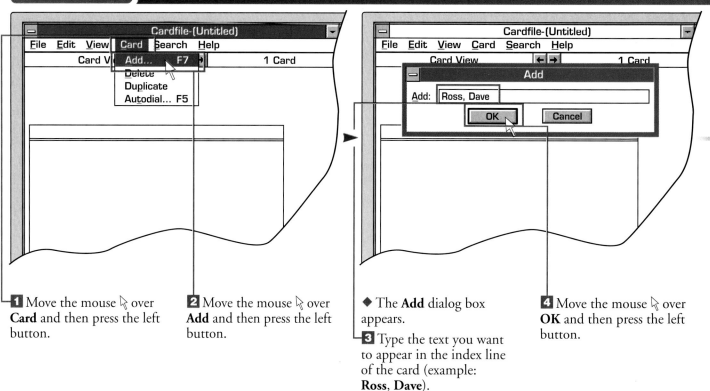

1 Move the mouse ⇖ over **Card** and then press the left button.

2 Move the mouse ⇖ over **Add** and then press the left button.

◆ The **Add** dialog box appears.

3 Type the text you want to appear in the index line of the card (example: **Ross, Dave**).

4 Move the mouse ⇖ over **OK** and then press the left button.

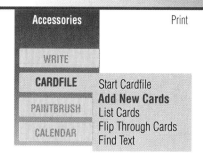

| Accessories | Print | Control Panel | Run DOS in Windows | Sharing Data | Improve Windows Performance |

WRITE

CARDFILE — Start Cardfile
Add New Cards
List Cards
Flip Through Cards
Find Text

PAINTBRUSH

CALENDAR

DELETE A CARD

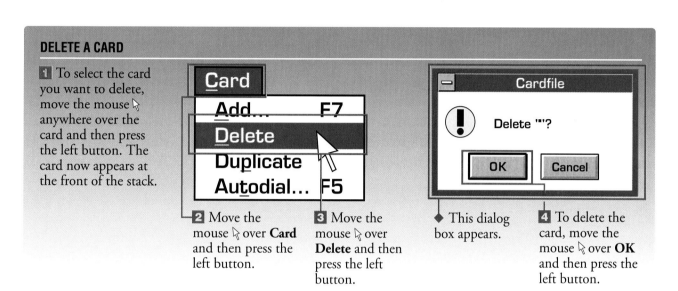

1 To select the card you want to delete, move the mouse �️ anywhere over the card and then press the left button. The card now appears at the front of the stack.

2 Move the mouse �️ over **Card** and then press the left button.

3 Move the mouse �️ over **Delete** and then press the left button.

◆ This dialog box appears.

4 To delete the card, move the mouse �️ over **OK** and then press the left button.

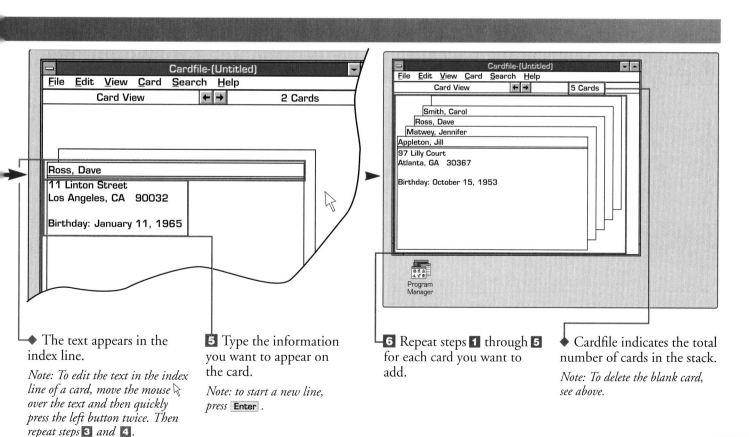

◆ The text appears in the index line.

*Note: To edit the text in the index line of a card, move the mouse �️ over the text and then quickly press the left button twice. Then repeat steps **3** and **4**.*

5 Type the information you want to appear on the card.

Note: to start a new line, press `Enter`.

6 Repeat steps **1** through **5** for each card you want to add.

◆ Cardfile indicates the total number of cards in the stack.

Note: To delete the blank card, see above.

143

LIST CARDS

FLIP THROUGH CARDS

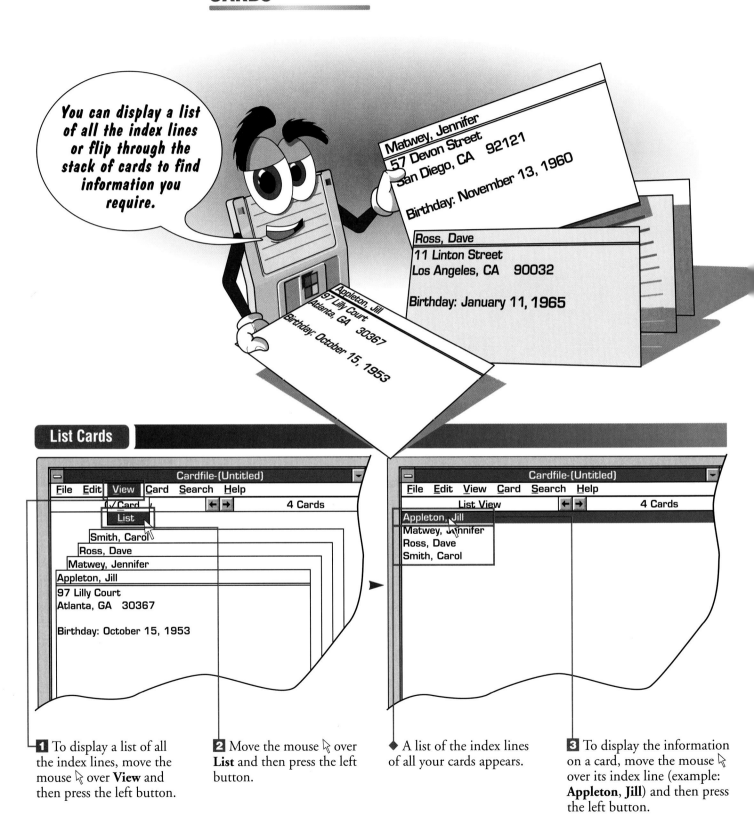

You can display a list of all the index lines or flip through the stack of cards to find information you require.
Matwey, Jennifer
57 Devon Street
San Diego, CA 92121
Birthday: November 13, 1960
Ross, Dave
11 Linton Street
Los Angeles, CA 90032
Birthday: January 11, 1965
Appleton, Jill
97 Lilly Court
Atlanta, GA 30367
Birthday: October 15, 1953

List Cards

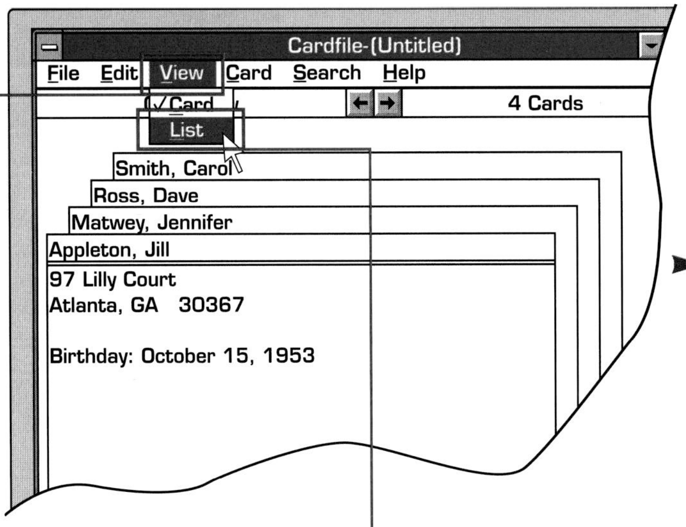

Cardfile-(Untitled)
File Edit View Card Search Help
√Card
List
4 Cards
Smith, Carol
Ross, Dave
Matwey, Jennifer
Appleton, Jill
97 Lilly Court
Atlanta, GA 30367
Birthday: October 15, 1953

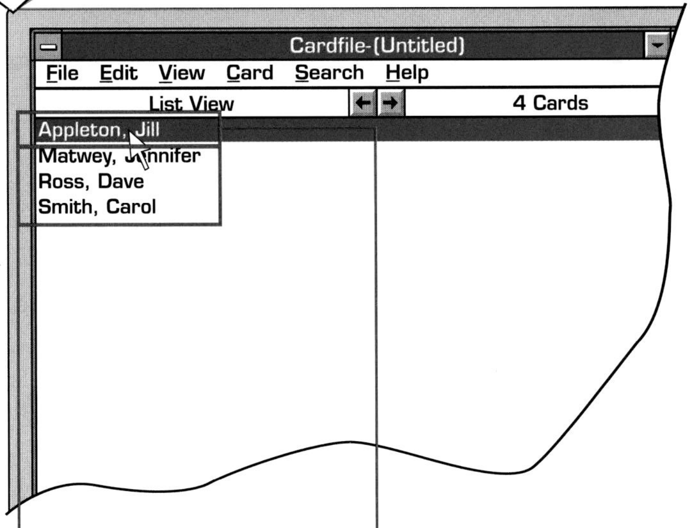

Cardfile-(Untitled)
File Edit View Card Search Help
List View
4 Cards
Appleton, Jill
Ross, Dave
Smith, Carol

1 To display a list of all the index lines, move the mouse over **View** and then press the left button.

2 Move the mouse over **List** and then press the left button.

◆ A list of the index lines of all your cards appears.

3 To display the information on a card, move the mouse over its index line (example: **Appleton, Jill**) and then press the left button.

4 Repeat step **1** and then select **Card** in step **2**.

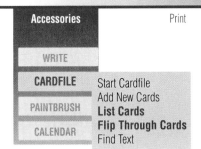

| Accessories | Print | Control Panel | Run DOS in Windows | Sharing Data | Improve Windows Performance |

WRITE

CARDFILE — Start Cardfile
Add New Cards
List Cards
Flip Through Cards
Find Text

PAINTBRUSH

CALENDAR

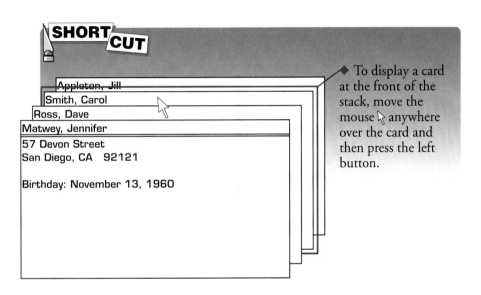

SHORT CUT

Appleton, Jill
Smith, Carol
Ross, Dave
Matwey, Jennifer
57 Devon Street
San Diego, CA   92121

Birthday: November 13, 1960

◆ To display a card at the front of the stack, move the mouse anywhere over the card and then press the left button.

Flip Through Cards

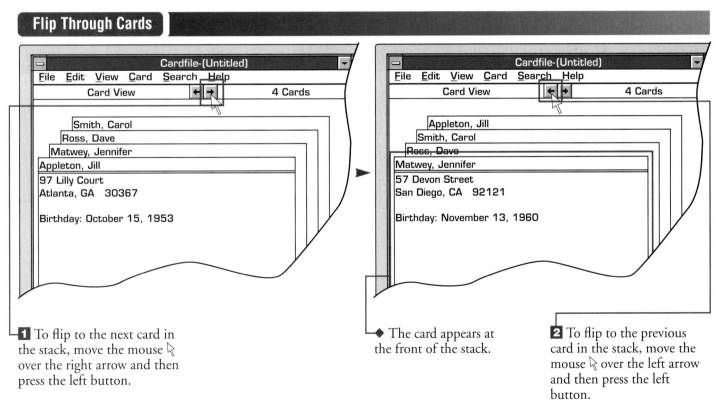

1 To flip to the next card in the stack, move the mouse over the right arrow and then press the left button.

◆ The card appears at the front of the stack.

2 To flip to the previous card in the stack, move the mouse over the left arrow and then press the left button.

145

FIND
TEXT

You can search for a specific word or phrase in your stack of cards. The first card containing the text will appear at the front of the stack.

Find Text

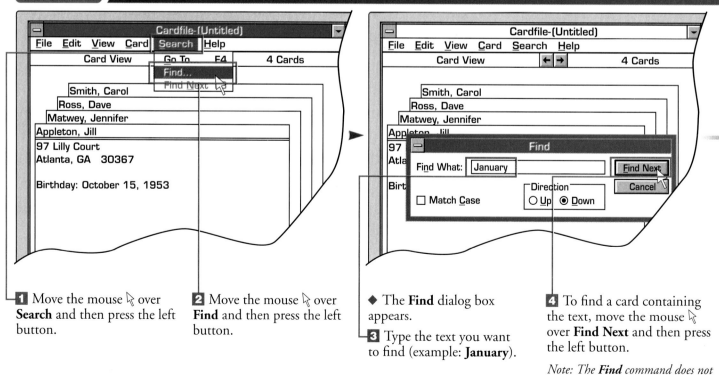

1 Move the mouse ⬉ over **Search** and then press the left button.

2 Move the mouse ⬉ over **Find** and then press the left button.

◆ The **Find** dialog box appears.

3 Type the text you want to find (example: **January**).

4 To find a card containing the text, move the mouse ⬉ over **Find Next** and then press the left button.

*Note: The **Find** command does not search the index lines of the cards.*

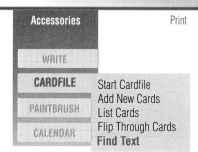

| Accessories | Print | Control Panel | Run DOS in Windows | Sharing Data | Improve Windows Performance |

WRITE

CARDFILE
- Start Cardfile
- Add New Cards

PAINTBRUSH
- List Cards
- Flip Through Cards

CALENDAR
- **Find Text**

SAVE YOUR WORK

You must save your work to permanently store it for future use.

*Note: To save your work, refer to page 128. Cardfile automatically adds the **CRD** extension to its files.*

EXIT CARDFILE

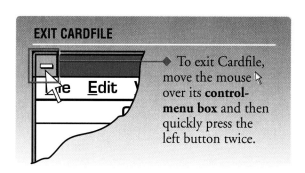

◆ To exit Cardfile, move the mouse over its **control-menu box** and then quickly press the left button twice.

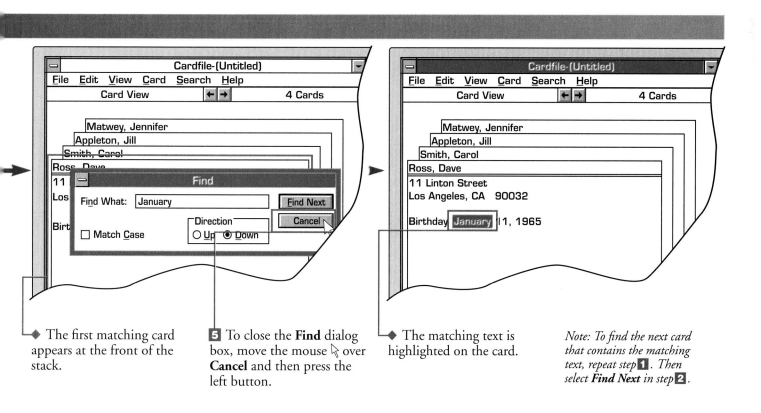

◆ The first matching card appears at the front of the stack.

5 To close the **Find** dialog box, move the mouse over **Cancel** and then press the left button.

◆ The matching text is highlighted on the card.

*Note: To find the next card that contains the matching text, repeat step **1**. Then select **Find Next** in step **2**.*

START
PAINTBRUSH

Paintbrush is a program that enables you to make use of your artistic abilities. For example, you can create illustrations, maps and signs on your computer.

Start Paintbrush

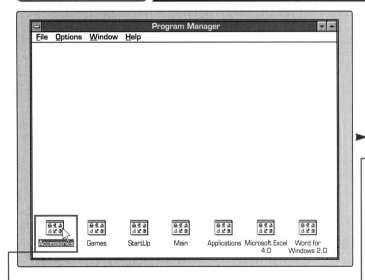

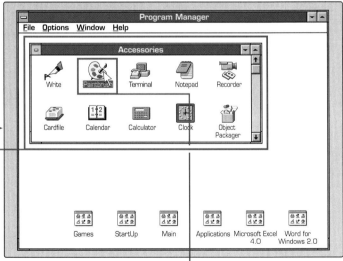

1 To open the **Accessories** group window, move the mouse ⬚ over its icon and then quickly press the left button twice.

◆ The **Accessories** group window opens.

2 To start the **Paintbrush** program, move the mouse ⬚ over its icon and then quickly press the left button twice.

WRITE

CARDFILE

PAINTBRUSH

CALENDAR

Start Paintbrush
Draw Lines
Draw Shapes
Type Text
Use the Eraser
Move a Drawing

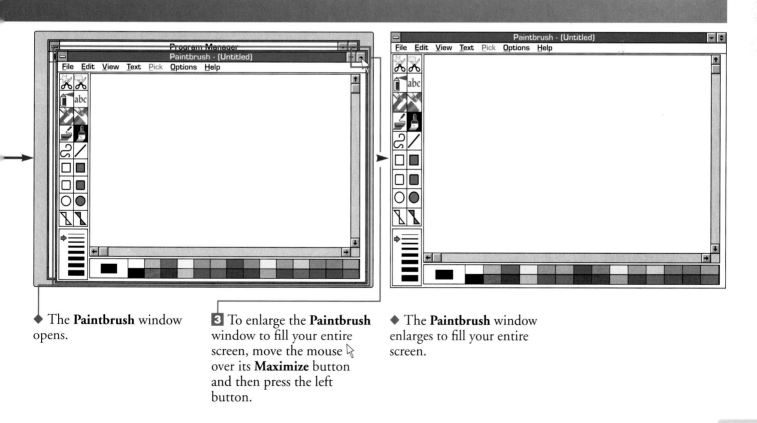

◆ The **Paintbrush** window opens.

3 To enlarge the **Paintbrush** window to fill your entire screen, move the mouse over its **Maximize** button and then press the left button.

◆ The **Paintbrush** window enlarges to fill your entire screen.

DRAW LINES

Paintbrush provides you with tools to draw wavy and straight lines. You can use any color displayed at the bottom of your screen.

Draw Lines

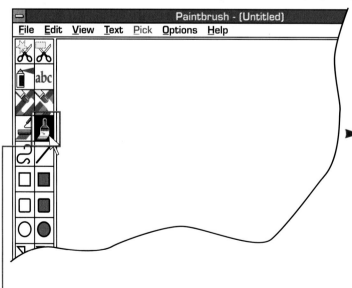

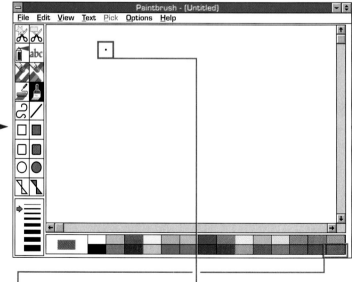

1 Move the mouse ⊾ over the line tool you want to use (example: 🖌) and then press the left button.

◆ The mouse ⊾ changes to (•) when you move it over the drawing area.

2 To select a color for the line, move the mouse ⊾ over the color you want to use and then press the left button.

3 Move the mouse (•) where you want to begin drawing the line.

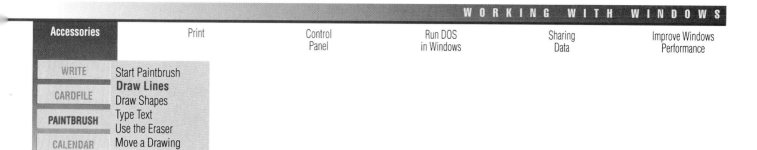

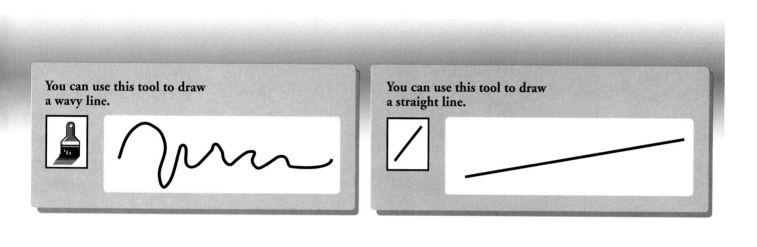

You can use this tool to draw a wavy line.

You can use this tool to draw a straight line.

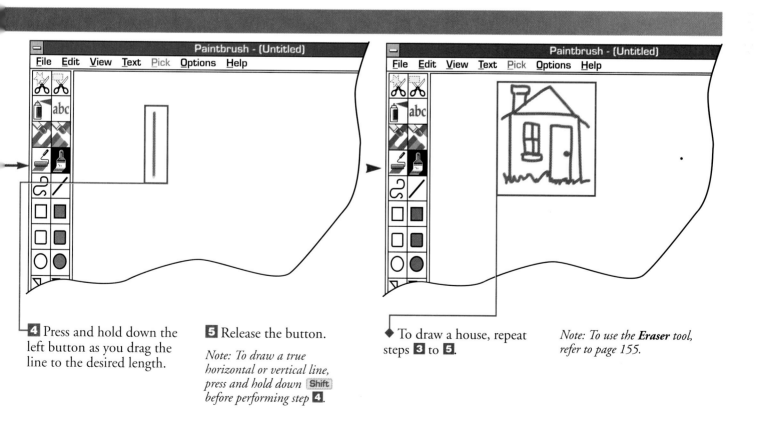

4 Press and hold down the left button as you drag the line to the desired length.

5 Release the button.

Note: To draw a true horizontal or vertical line, press and hold down Shift *before performing step* **4**.

◆ To draw a house, repeat steps **3** to **5**.

*Note: To use the **Eraser** tool, refer to page 155.*

DRAW SHAPES

You can draw a box, circle or ellipse using any color displayed at the bottom of your screen.

Draw Shapes

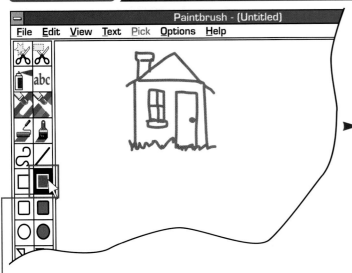

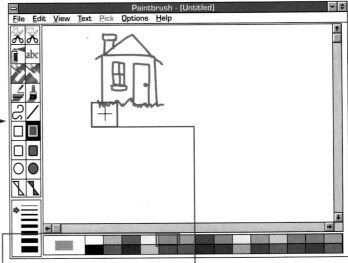

1 Move the mouse ⌖ over the shape icon you want to use (example: ▣) and then press the left button.

◆ The mouse ⌖ changes to ✛ when you move it over the drawing area.

2 To select a color for the shape, move the mouse ⌖ over the color you want to use and then press the left button.

3 Move the mouse ✛ where you want the top left corner of the shape to appear.

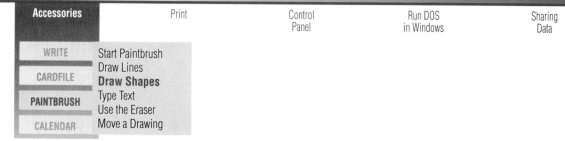

Accessories | Print | Control Panel | Run DOS in Windows | Sharing Data | Improve Windows Performance

WRITE

CARDFILE

PAINTBRUSH

CALENDAR

Start Paintbrush
Draw Lines
Draw Shapes
Type Text
Use the Eraser
Move a Drawing

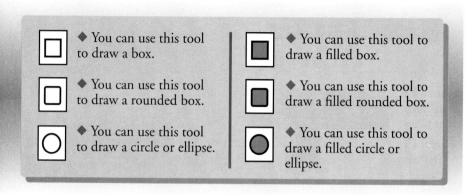

◆ You can use this tool to draw a box.

◆ You can use this tool to draw a filled box.

◆ You can use this tool to draw a rounded box.

◆ You can use this tool to draw a filled rounded box.

◆ You can use this tool to draw a circle or ellipse.

◆ You can use this tool to draw a filled circle or ellipse.

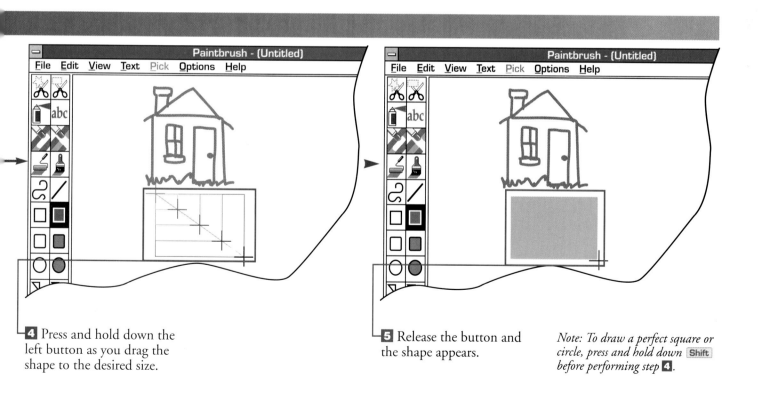

4 Press and hold down the left button as you drag the shape to the desired size.

5 Release the button and the shape appears.

Note: To draw a perfect square or circle, press and hold down Shift *before performing step* **4**.

TYPE TEXT

USE THE ERASER

You can use the Text tool to add titles and explanations to your drawings.

 **Type Text**

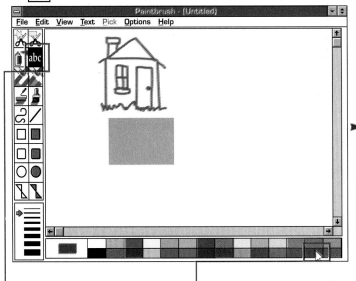

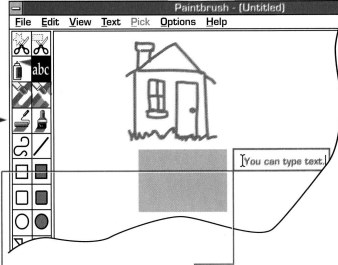

1 Move the mouse ⬚ over the **Text** tool and then press the left button.

◆ The mouse ⬚ changes to I when you move it over the drawing area.

2 Move the mouse ⬚ over the color you want the text to appear as and then press the left button.

3 Move the mouse I where you want the text to appear and then press the left button.

4 Type the text.

Note: If you make a typing error, press **←Backspace** *to remove the incorrect text and then retype.*

154

| Accessories | Print | Control Panel | Run DOS in Windows | Sharing Data | Improve Windows Performance |

You can use the Eraser tool to remove all or part of your drawing.

Use the Eraser

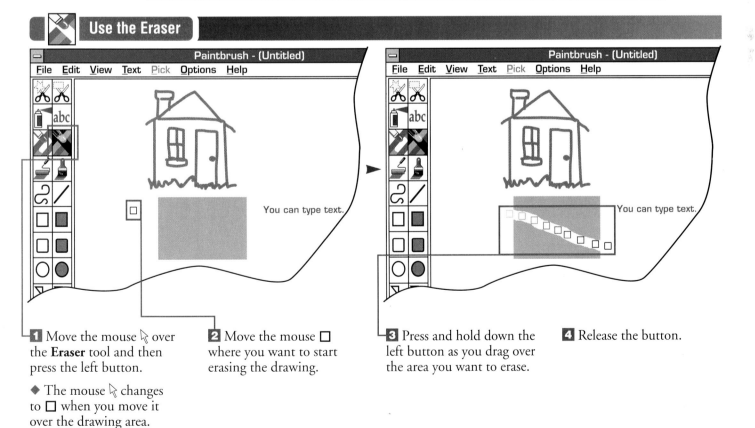

1 Move the mouse ⇧ over the **Eraser** tool and then press the left button.

◆ The mouse ⇧ changes to □ when you move it over the drawing area.

2 Move the mouse □ where you want to start erasing the drawing.

3 Press and hold down the left button as you drag over the area you want to erase.

4 Release the button.

MOVE A DRAWING

You can move a drawing to a new location on your screen.

Move a Drawing

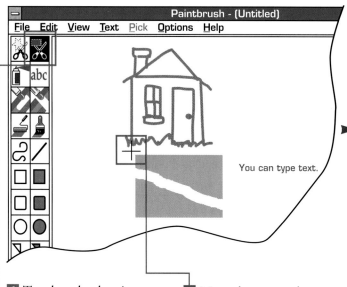

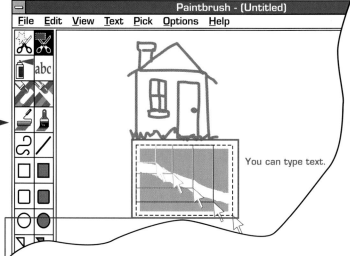

1 To select the drawing you want to move, place the mouse ▷ over the **Pick** tool and then press the left button.

◆ The mouse ▷ changes to + when you move it over the drawing area.

2 Move the mouse + over the top left corner of the drawing you want to move.

3 Press and hold down the left button as you drag the mouse until a box completely surrounds the drawing.

4 Release the button.

Note: The dashed line remains.

| Accessories | Print | Control Panel | Run DOS in Windows | Sharing Data | Improve Windows Performance |

WRITE
CARDFILE
PAINTBRUSH
CALENDAR

Start Paintbrush
Draw Lines
Draw Shapes
Type Text
Use the Eraser
Move a Drawing

SAVE YOUR DRAWING

You must save your drawing to permanently store it for future use.

*Note: To save your drawing, refer to page 128. Paintbrush automatically adds the **BMP** extension to its files.*

EXIT PAINTBRUSH

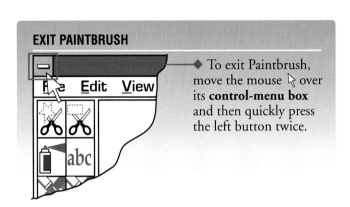

File   Edit   View

◆ To exit Paintbrush, move the mouse ⬀ over its **control-menu box** and then quickly press the left button twice.

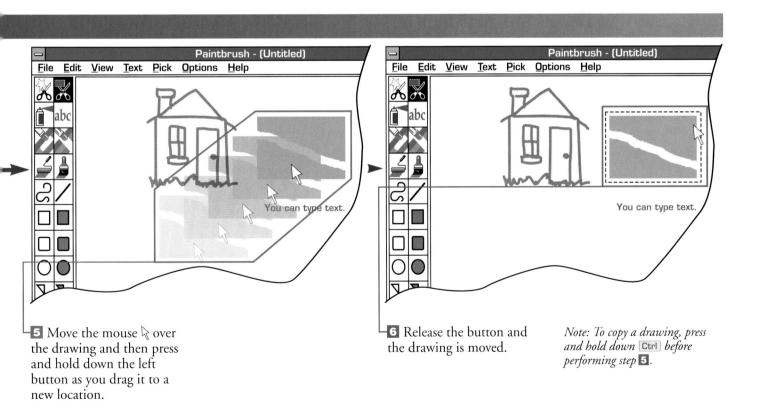

5 Move the mouse ⬀ over the drawing and then press and hold down the left button as you drag it to a new location.

6 Release the button and the drawing is moved.

Note: To copy a drawing, press and hold down Ctrl *before performing step* **5**.

START
CALENDAR

Calendar helps you to stay organized by keeping track of your daily activities. You can use this program to record appointments and remind you of upcoming events.

Start Calendar

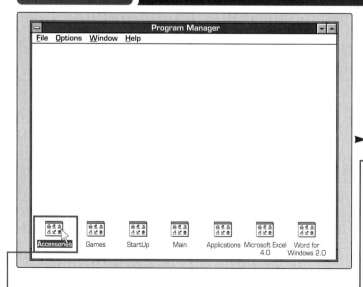

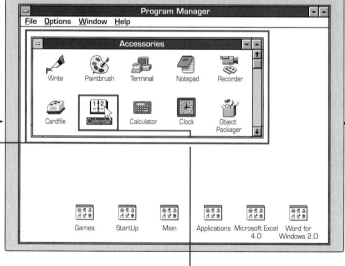

1 To open the **Accessories** group window, move the mouse ⌖ over its icon and then quickly press the left button twice.

◆ The **Accessories** group window opens.

2 To start the **Calendar** program, move the mouse ⌖ over its icon and then quickly press the left button twice.

| Accessories | Print | Control Panel | Run DOS in Windows | Sharing Data | Improve Windows Performance |

WRITE

CARDFILE

PAINTBRUSH

CALENDAR

Start Calendar
Display the Month View
Enter Appointments
Set Alarms

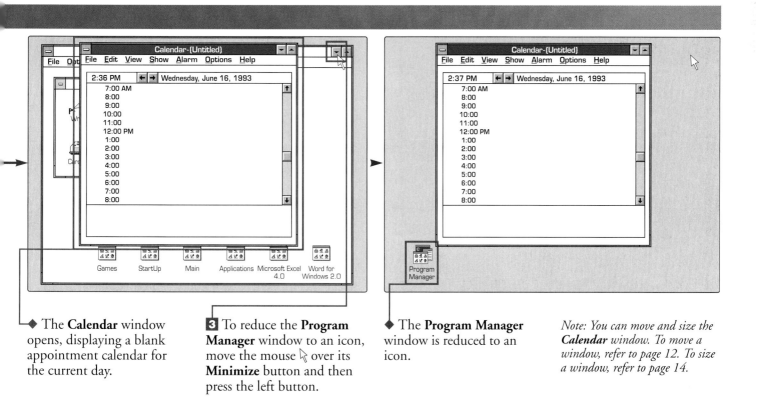

◆ The **Calendar** window opens, displaying a blank appointment calendar for the current day.

3 To reduce the **Program Manager** window to an icon, move the mouse ⬉ over its **Minimize** button and then press the left button.

◆ The **Program Manager** window is reduced to an icon.

*Note: You can move and size the **Calendar** window. To move a window, refer to page 12. To size a window, refer to page 14.*

DISPLAY THE MONTH VIEW

You can display all the days in a month on your screen. Calendar also enables you to flip through the months.

Display the Month View

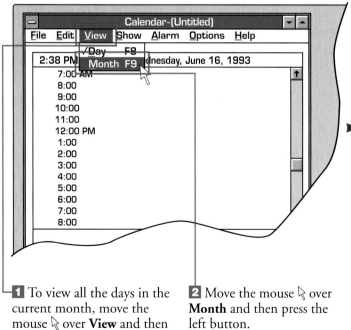

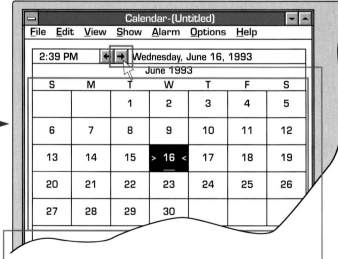

1 To view all the days in the current month, move the mouse Ⓚ over **View** and then press the left button.

2 Move the mouse ⓀⓀ over **Month** and then press the left button.

◆ The days in the current month are displayed.

Note: The current day displays the > < symbols.

3 To display the next month, move the mouse ⓀⓀ over this arrow and then press the left button.

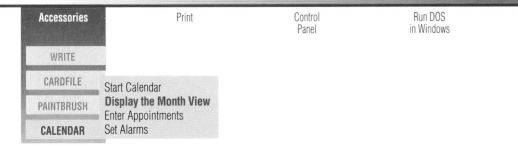

WRITE

CARDFILE

PAINTBRUSH

CALENDAR

Start Calendar
Display the Month View
Enter Appointments
Set Alarms

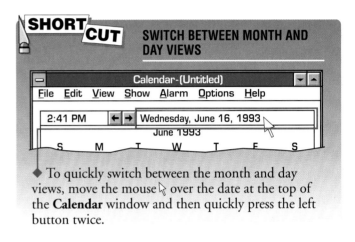

SHORT**CUT**

SWITCH BETWEEN MONTH AND DAY VIEWS

◆ To quickly switch between the month and day views, move the mouse ⬚ over the date at the top of the **Calendar** window and then quickly press the left button twice.

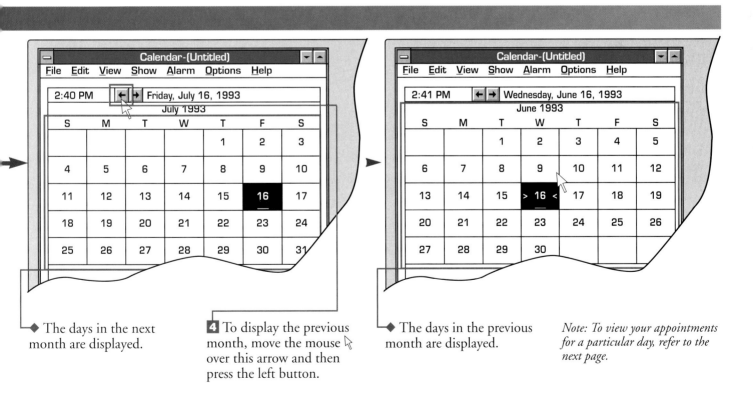

◆ The days in the next month are displayed.

4 To display the previous month, move the mouse ⬚ over this arrow and then press the left button.

◆ The days in the previous month are displayed.

Note: To view your appointments for a particular day, refer to the next page.

ENTER
APPOINTMENTS

The Calendar enables you to keep track of appointments and provides you with an area to enter miscellaneous notes.

Enter Appointments

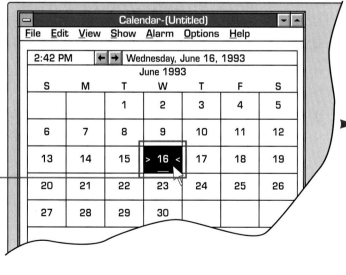

1 To view your appointments for a particular day, move the mouse ⌖ over the day (example: **16**) and then quickly press the left button twice.

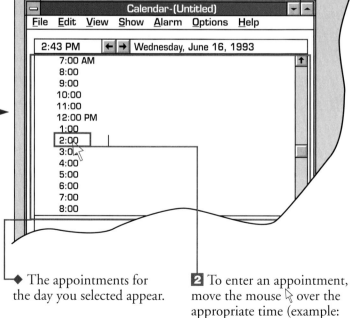

◆ The appointments for the day you selected appear.

2 To enter an appointment, move the mouse ⌖ over the appropriate time (example: **2:00**) and then press the left button.

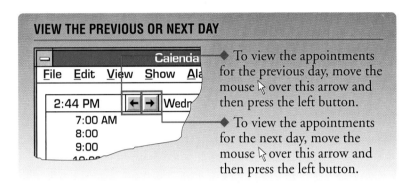

VIEW THE PREVIOUS OR NEXT DAY

◆ To view the appointments for the previous day, move the mouse ☐ over this arrow and then press the left button.

◆ To view the appointments for the next day, move the mouse ☐ over this arrow and then press the left button.

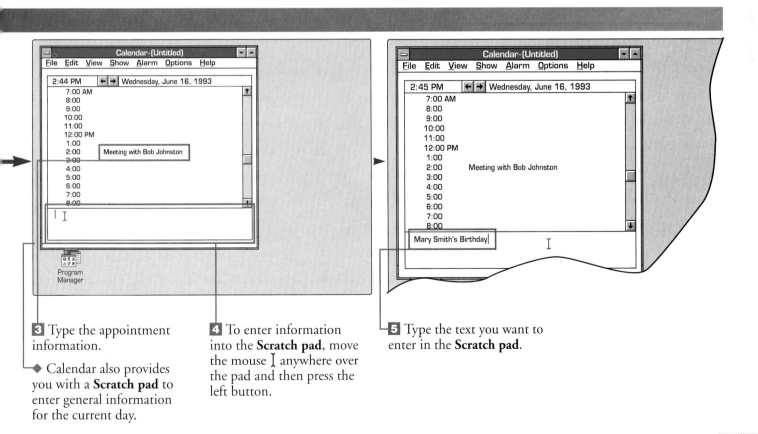

3 Type the appointment information.

◆ Calendar also provides you with a **Scratch pad** to enter general information for the current day.

4 To enter information into the **Scratch pad**, move the mouse ☐ anywhere over the pad and then press the left button.

5 Type the text you want to enter in the **Scratch pad**.

SET
ALARMS

You can set alarms at different times during the day to remind you of important activities or meetings.

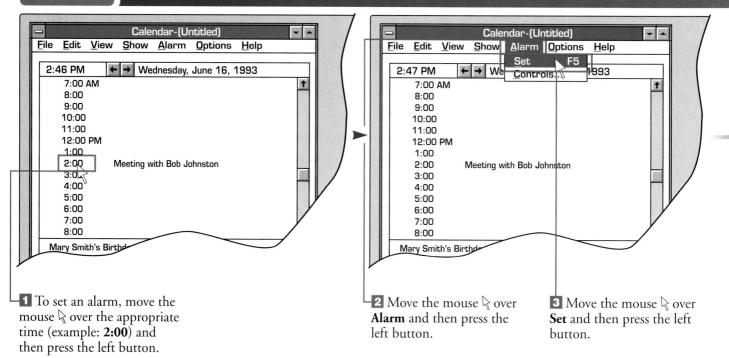

1 To set an alarm, move the mouse ▷ over the appropriate time (example: **2:00**) and then press the left button.

2 Move the mouse ▷ over **Alarm** and then press the left button.

3 Move the mouse ▷ over **Set** and then press the left button.

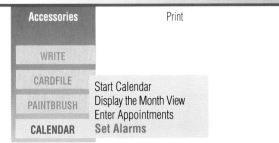

| Accessories | Print | Control Panel | Run DOS in Windows | Sharing Data | Improve Windows Performance |

WRITE

CARDFILE — Start Calendar
PAINTBRUSH — Display the Month View
— Enter Appointments
CALENDAR — **Set Alarms**

IMPORTANT

For alarms to work:

◆ The Calendar file containing the alarm settings must be open. Make sure you open this file each time you start Windows.

◆ The date and time set in your computer must correspond to the present date and time.

Note: To open a file, refer to page 130. To check the date and time set in your computer, refer to page 180.

SAVE YOUR WORK

You must save your work to permanently store it for future use.

Note: To save your work, refer to page 128. Calendar automatically adds the **CAL** *extension to its files.*

EXIT CALENDAR

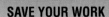

◆ To exit Calendar, move the mouse ⬚ over its **control-menu box** and then quickly press the left button twice.

◆ A bell appears next to the time.

Note: You can remove the alarm by repeating steps 1 to 3.

When the set time arrives, you will hear four beeps and a dialog box will appear reminding you of the appointment.

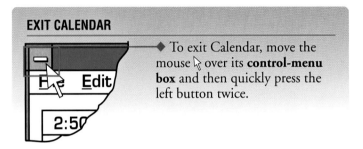

◆ To close the dialog box, move the mouse ⬚ over **OK** and then press the left button.

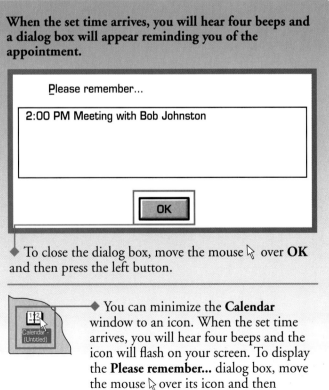

◆ You can minimize the **Calendar** window to an icon. When the set time arrives, you will hear four beeps and the icon will flash on your screen. To display the **Please remember...** dialog box, move the mouse ⬚ over its icon and then quickly press the left button twice.

PRINT
A FILE

> You can use the Print command to produce a paper copy of a document displayed on your screen.

PRINTER MODE: ON – PROCESSING

Print a File

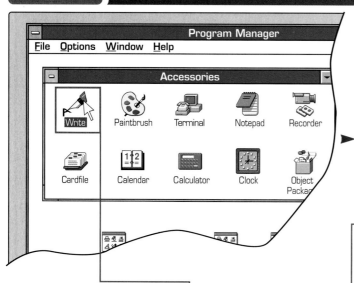

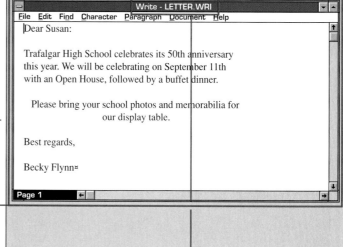

1 Start the application containing the document you want to print (example: **Write**).

◆ To start the **Write** application, move the mouse ⬦ over its icon and then quickly press the left button twice.

◆ The **Write** window opens.

2 Move and size the window as shown above.

Note: To move a window, refer to page 12. To size a window, refer to page 14.

3 Open the document you want to print (example: **LETTER.WRI**).

Note: To open a document, refer to page 130.

Print a File
Change Print Setup
Cancel a Print Job
Pause a Print Job
Change Print Order
Start the Print Manager
Drag and Drop Printing

TIP

Print Manager

◆ When you print a document, the **Print Manager** icon appears at the bottom of your screen. The icon disappears when the printing is complete.

The **Print Manager** controls the printing of your documents. It enables you to cancel or pause printing.

Note: For more information, refer to pages 170 to 172.

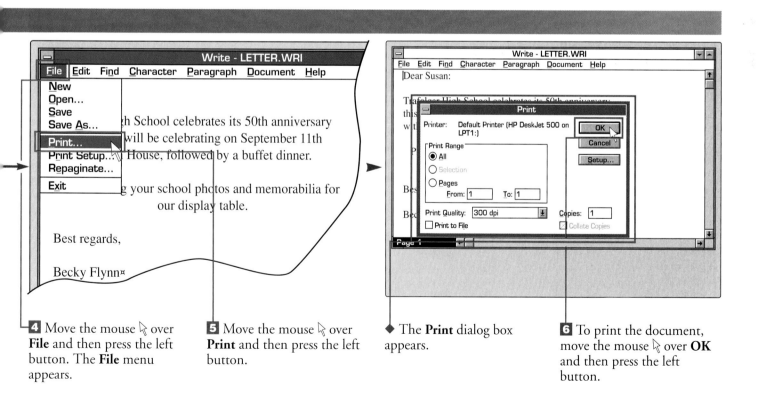

4 Move the mouse ⇧ over **File** and then press the left button. The **File** menu appears.

5 Move the mouse ⇧ over **Print** and then press the left button.

◆ The **Print** dialog box appears.

6 To print the document, move the mouse ⇧ over **OK** and then press the left button.

CHANGE PRINT SETUP

If your computer is connected to more than one printer, you can easily switch to the one you want to use.

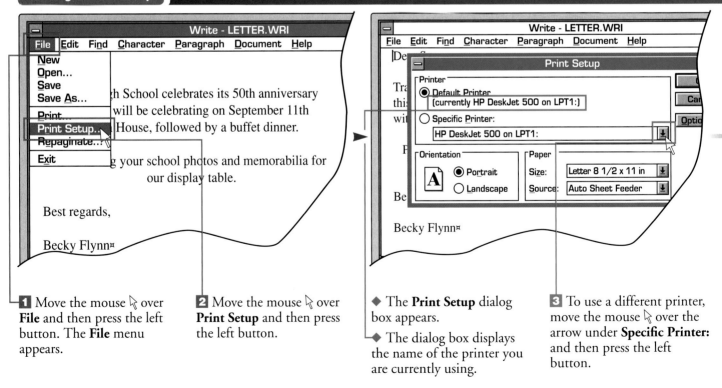

1 Move the mouse ⬦ over **File** and then press the left button. The **File** menu appears.

2 Move the mouse ⬦ over **Print Setup** and then press the left button.

◆ The **Print Setup** dialog box appears.

◆ The dialog box displays the name of the printer you are currently using.

3 To use a different printer, move the mouse ⬦ over the arrow under **Specific Printer:** and then press the left button.

Accessories   **Print**   Control Panel   Run DOS in Windows   Sharing Data   Improve Windows Performance

Print a File
Change Print Setup
Cancel a Print Job
Pause a Print Job
Change Print Order
Start the Print Manager
Drag and Drop Printing

CHANGE PAGE ORIENTATION

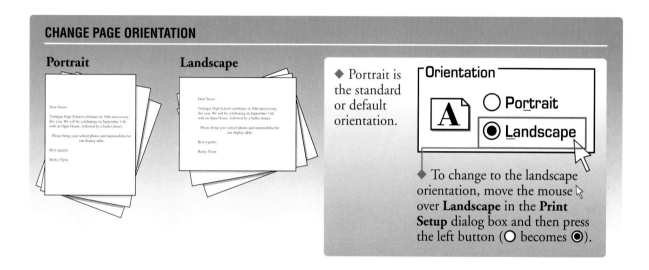

Portrait

Landscape

◆ Portrait is the standard or default orientation.

Orientation

○ Po**r**trait

◉ **L**andscape

◆ To change to the landscape orientation, move the mouse ⍐ over **Landscape** in the **Print Setup** dialog box and then press the left button (○ becomes ◉).

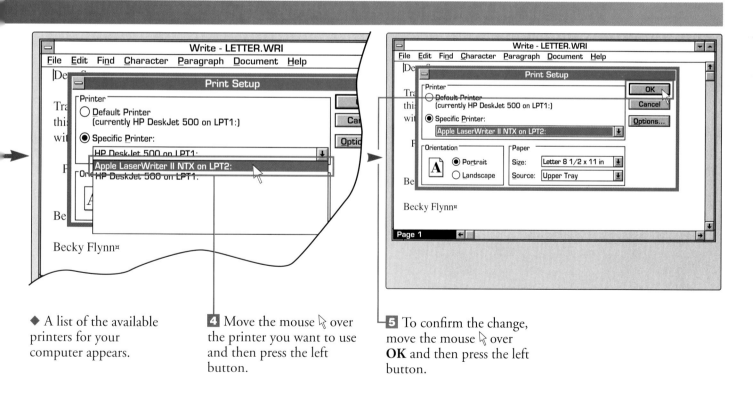

◆ A list of the available printers for your computer appears.

4 Move the mouse ⍐ over the printer you want to use and then press the left button.

5 To confirm the change, move the mouse ⍐ over **OK** and then press the left button.

CANCEL A PRINT JOB

If you accidentally sent a document twice to the printer, you can use the Print Manager to cancel the print job.

Cancel a Print Job

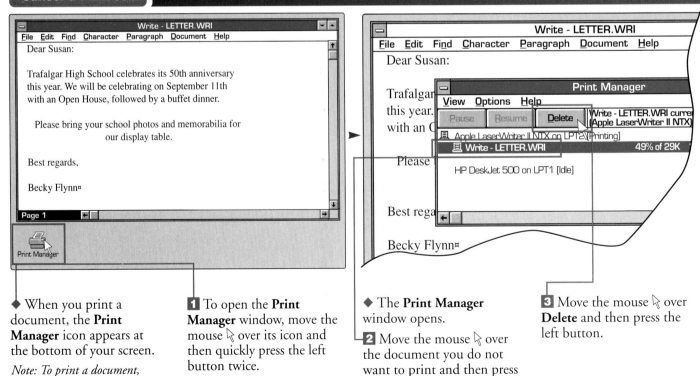

◆ When you print a document, the **Print Manager** icon appears at the bottom of your screen.

Note: To print a document, refer to page 166.

1 To open the **Print Manager** window, move the mouse ⟍ over its icon and then quickly press the left button twice.

◆ The **Print Manager** window opens.

2 Move the mouse ⟍ over the document you do not want to print and then press the left button.

3 Move the mouse ⟍ over **Delete** and then press the left button.

Accessories   **Print**   Control   Run DOS   Sharing   Improve Windows
                                         Panel   in Windows   Data   Performance

Print a File
Change Print Setup
Cancel a Print Job
Pause a Print Job
Change Print Order
Start the Print Manager
Drag and Drop Printing

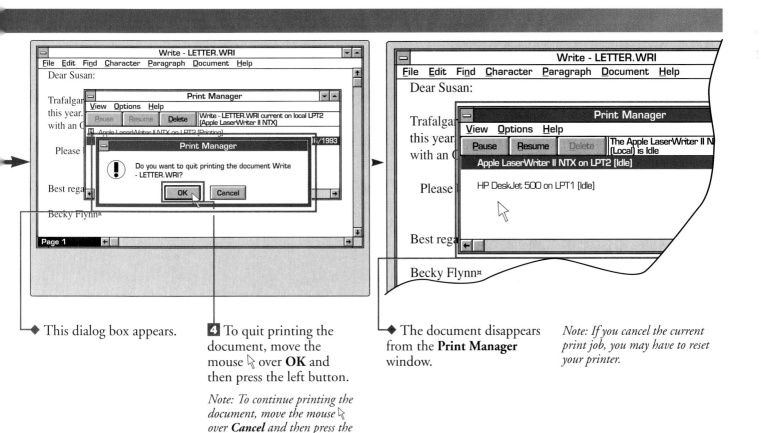

◆ This dialog box appears.

4 To quit printing the document, move the mouse ⌖ over **OK** and then press the left button.

*Note: To continue printing the document, move the mouse ⌖ over **Cancel** and then press the left button.*

◆ The document disappears from the **Print Manager** window.

Note: If you cancel the current print job, you may have to reset your printer.

Pause a Print Job

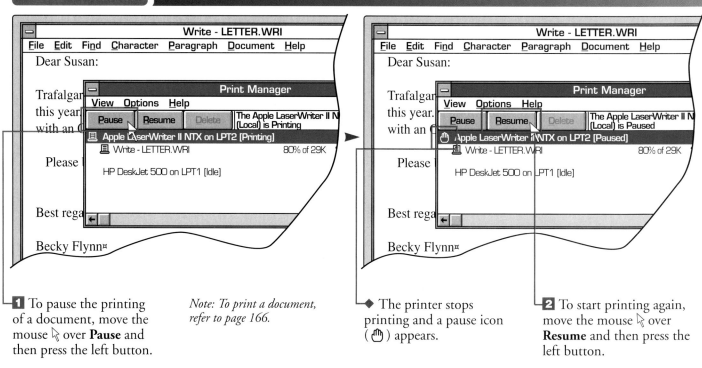

1 To pause the printing of a document, move the mouse ⌖ over **Pause** and then press the left button.

Note: To print a document, refer to page 166.

◆ The printer stops printing and a pause icon (🖑) appears.

2 To start printing again, move the mouse ⌖ over **Resume** and then press the left button.

Accessories	**Print**	Control Panel	Run DOS in Windows	Sharing Data	Improve Windows Performance

Print a File
Change Print Setup
Cancel a Print Job
Pause a Print Job
Change Print Order
Start the Print Manager
Drag and Drop Printing

IMPORTANT

You cannot change the print order of the job currently printing.

Change Print Order

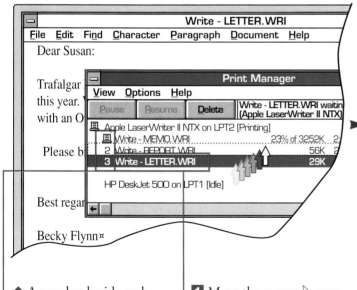

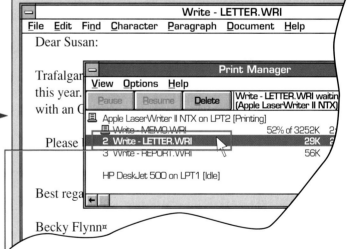

◆ A number beside each document indicates the print order. The job currently printing displays the 🖳 symbol.

1 Move the mouse ⍾ over the document you want to reposition.

2 Press and hold down the left button as you drag the document to the new position.

3 Release the button and the document moves.

Note: In this example, the document was moved from the third to the second position and will be the next document printed.

START THE PRINT MANAGER

You can have the Print Manager program running all the time. This enables you to print documents directly from the File Manager without having to open the application that created them.

Print Manager

View Options Help

| Pause | Resume | Delete |

The App... ...rite (Local) is Id...

Apple LaserWriter II NTX on LPT2 [Idle]

HP DeskJet 500 on LPT1 [Idle]

Start the Print Manager

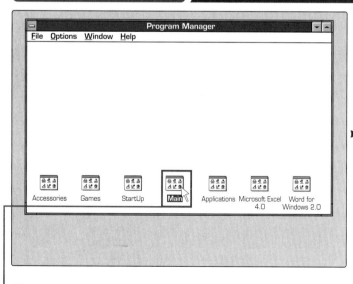

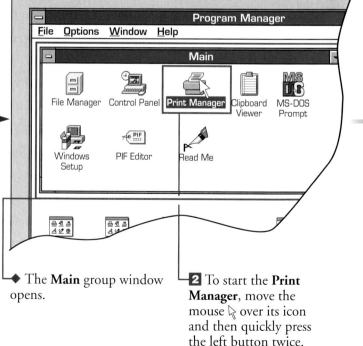

1 To open the **Main** group window, move the mouse ⌖ over its icon and then quickly press the left button twice.

◆ The **Main** group window opens.

2 To start the **Print Manager**, move the mouse ⌖ over its icon and then quickly press the left button twice.

Accessories | **Print** | Control Panel | Run DOS in Windows | Sharing Data | Improve Windows Performance

Print a File
Change Print Setup
Cancel a Print Job
Pause a Print Job
Change Print Order
Start the Print Manager
Drag and Drop Printing

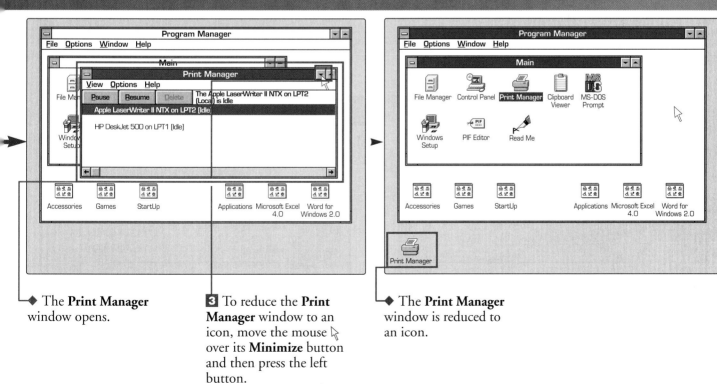

◆ The **Print Manager** window opens.

3 To reduce the **Print Manager** window to an icon, move the mouse over its **Minimize** button and then press the left button.

◆ The **Print Manager** window is reduced to an icon.

DRAG AND DROP PRINTING

You can print a document directly from the File Manager. This can save you time since you do not have to open the application that created the file.

Print a File from the File Manager

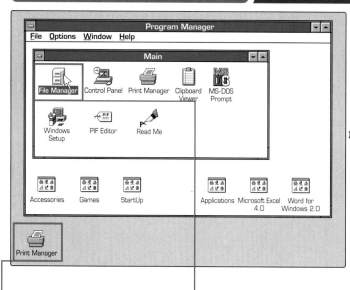

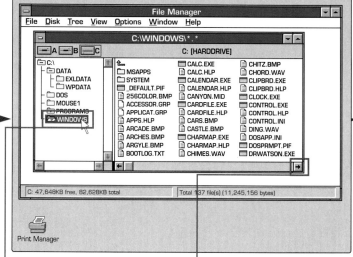

1 Start the **Print Manager** and display it as an icon at the bottom of your screen.

Note: To start the Print Manager, refer to page 174.

2 To open the **File Manager**, move the mouse ⌖ over its icon and then quickly press the left button twice.

◆ The **File Manager** window opens.

3 Move the mouse ⌖ over the directory containing the file you want to print (example: **WINDOWS**) and then press the left button.

4 To view more files in the current directory, move the mouse ⌖ over this arrow and then press the left button.

| Accessories | **Print** | Control Panel | Run DOS in Windows | Sharing Data | Improve Windows Performance |

Print a File
Change Print Setup
Cancel a Print Job
Pause a Print Job
Change Print Order
Start the Print Manager
Drag and Drop Printing

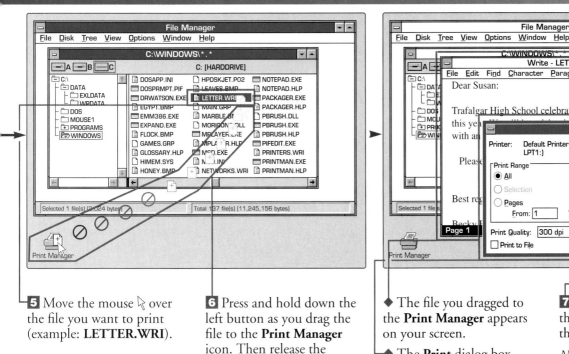

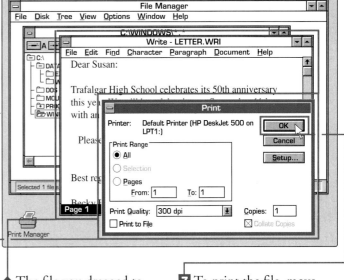

5 Move the mouse ⊮ over the file you want to print (example: **LETTER.WRI**).

6 Press and hold down the left button as you drag the file to the **Print Manager** icon. Then release the button.

◆ The file you dragged to the **Print Manager** appears on your screen.

◆ The **Print** dialog box also appears.

7 To print the file, move the mouse ⊮ over **OK** and then press the left button.

*Note: To cancel the printing, move the mouse ⊮ over **Cancel** and then press the left button.*

OPEN THE CONTROL PANEL

You can use the Control Panel to change the Windows environment. The Control Panel enables you to:

◆ change the current date and time set in your computer

◆ change the colors and patterns displayed on your screen

◆ use a screen saver

◆ change the mouse settings

◆ install fonts

Open the Control Panel

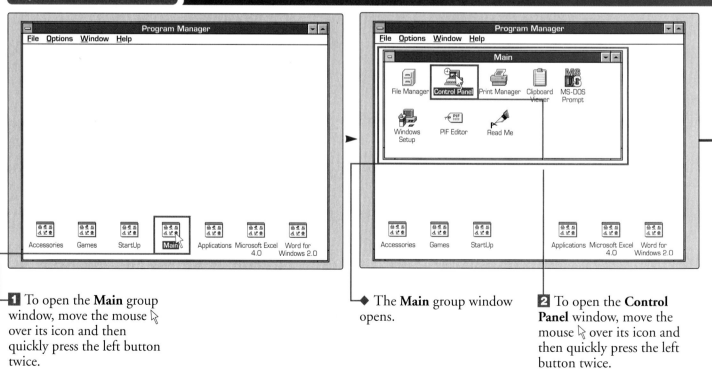

1 To open the **Main** group window, move the mouse ⬦ over its icon and then quickly press the left button twice.

◆ The **Main** group window opens.

2 To open the **Control Panel** window, move the mouse ⬦ over its icon and then quickly press the left button twice.

Open the Control Panel
Change Date and Time
Change Screen Colors
Add Wallpaper
Use a Screen Saver
Change Mouse Settings
Install Fonts

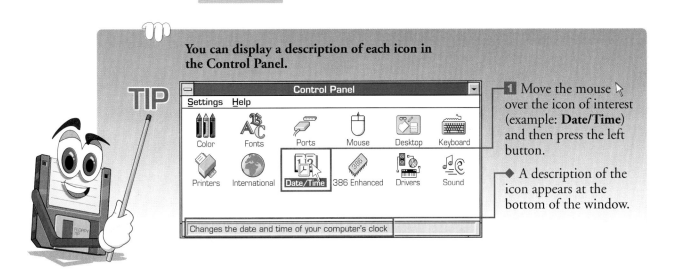

TIP

You can display a description of each icon in the Control Panel.

1 Move the mouse � over the icon of interest (example: **Date/Time**) and then press the left button.

◆ A description of the icon appears at the bottom of the window.

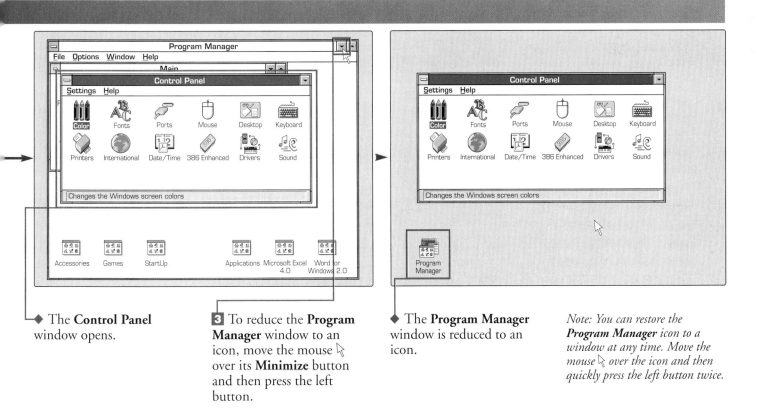

◆ The **Control Panel** window opens.

3 To reduce the **Program Manager** window to an icon, move the mouse ⍞ over its **Minimize** button and then press the left button.

◆ The **Program Manager** window is reduced to an icon.

*Note: You can restore the **Program Manager** icon to a window at any time. Move the mouse ⍞ over the icon and then quickly press the left button twice.*

CHANGE DATE AND TIME

You can change the date and time set in your computer. This is important if you want to save files using the correct date and time or if you are using time sensitive programs like Calendar.

Change Date and Time

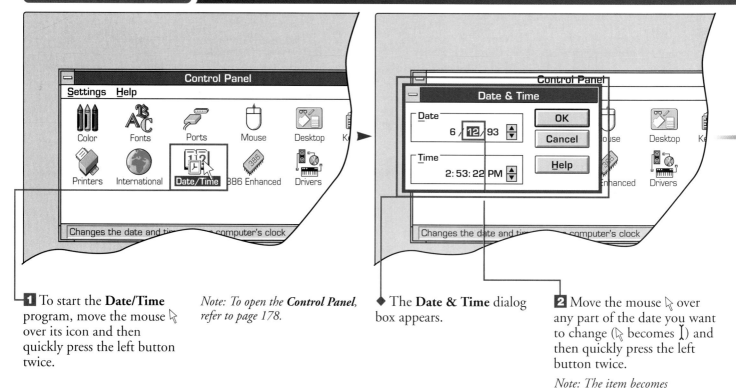

1 To start the **Date/Time** program, move the mouse ⌖ over its icon and then quickly press the left button twice.

*Note: To open the **Control Panel**, refer to page 178.*

◆ The **Date & Time** dialog box appears.

2 Move the mouse ⌖ over any part of the date you want to change (⌖ becomes I) and then quickly press the left button twice.

Note: The item becomes highlighted.

Open the Control Panel
Change Date and Time
Change Screen Colors
Add Wallpaper
Use a Screen Saver
Change Mouse Settings
Install Fonts

You can change any part of the date or time displayed in this dialog box.

◆ Month   ◆ Day   ◆ Year

Date & Time

Date
6 / 23 / 93

OK
Cancel
Help

Time
2: 10: 22 PM

◆ Hours   ◆ Minutes   ◆ Seconds   ◆ Period of the day (PM or AM)

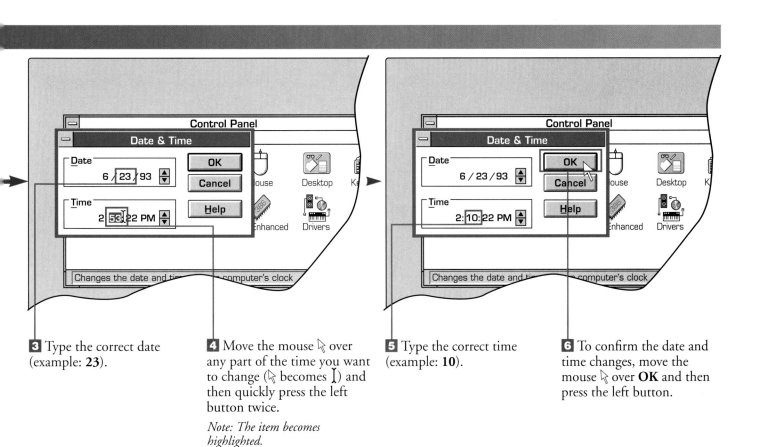

3 Type the correct date (example: **23**).

4 Move the mouse ⬉ over any part of the time you want to change (⬉ becomes Ɩ) and then quickly press the left button twice.

Note: The item becomes highlighted.

5 Type the correct time (example: **10**).

6 To confirm the date and time changes, move the mouse ⬉ over **OK** and then press the left button.

CHANGE SCREEN COLORS

You can change the colors that Windows displays on your screen. This can enhance the appearance of your desktop.

Change Screen Colors

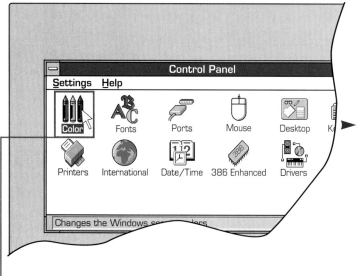

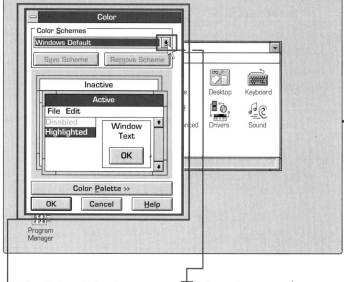

1 To start the **Color** program, move the mouse ⟲ over its icon and then quickly press the left button twice.

*Note: To open the **Control Panel**, refer to page 178.*

◆ The **Color** dialog box appears.

2 Move the mouse ⟲ over the arrow ⬇ under **Color Schemes** and then press the left button.

Accessories   Print   **Control Panel**   Run DOS in Windows   Sharing Data   Improve Windows Performance

Open the Control Panel
Change Date and Time
Change Screen Colors
Add Wallpaper
Use a Screen Saver
Change Mouse Settings
Install Fonts

TIP

If you have a portable computer with a monochrome screen, use one of the following color schemes:

LCD Default Screen Settings

LCD Reversed - Dark

LCD Reversed - Light

These color schemes provide maximum visibility.

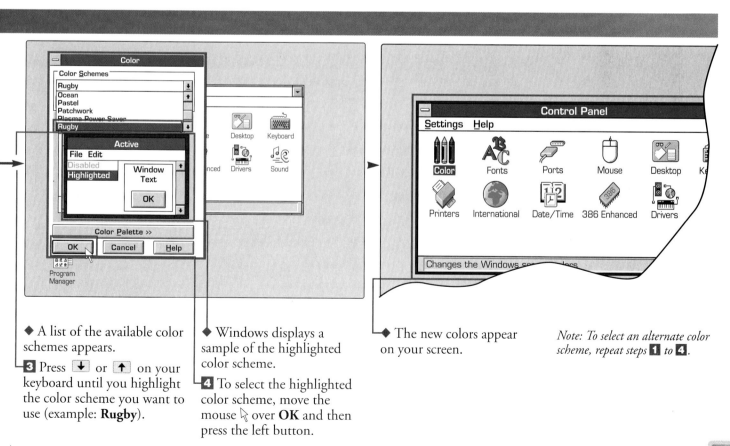

◆ A list of the available color schemes appears.

3 Press ⬇ or ⬆ on your keyboard until you highlight the color scheme you want to use (example: **Rugby**).

◆ Windows displays a sample of the highlighted color scheme.

4 To select the highlighted color scheme, move the mouse ⬉ over **OK** and then press the left button.

◆ The new colors appear on your screen.

*Note: To select an alternate color scheme, repeat steps **1** to **4**.*

ADD WALLPAPER

You can decorate your screen and impress your friends by using one of several wallpaper patterns offered by Windows.

Add Wallpaper

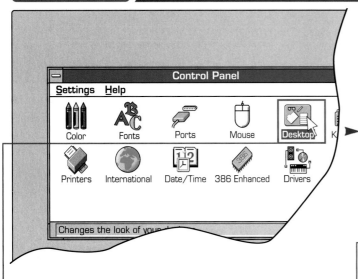

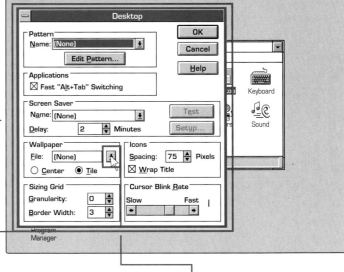

1 To start the **Desktop** program, move the mouse ⟍ over its icon and then quickly press the left button twice.

*Note: To open the **Control Panel**, refer to page 178.*

◆ The **Desktop** dialog box appears.

2 Move the mouse ⟍ over the arrow ⬇ under **Wallpaper** and then press the left button.

Accessories   Print   **Control
                                                 Panel**   Run DOS   Sharing   Improve Windows
                                                                                in Windows   Data   Performance

Open the Control Panel
Change Date and Time
Change Screen Colors
Add Wallpaper
Use a Screen Saver
Change Mouse Settings
Install Fonts

TIP

Displaying wallpaper on your screen reduces the memory available to run other applications. It may also slow down your computer.

If you start to run out of memory or your computer slows down, return to the **(None)** wallpaper option.

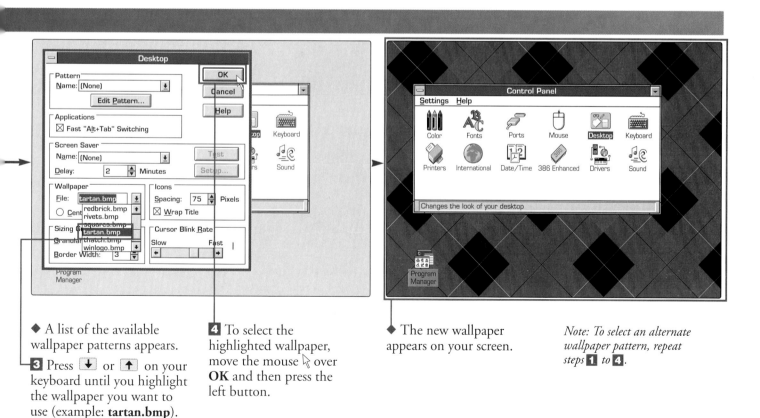

◆ A list of the available wallpaper patterns appears.

3 Press ⬇ or ⬆ on your keyboard until you highlight the wallpaper you want to use (example: **tartan.bmp**).

4 To select the highlighted wallpaper, move the mouse ⬉ over **OK** and then press the left button.

◆ The new wallpaper appears on your screen.

Note: To select an alternate wallpaper pattern, repeat steps **1** *to* **4**.

USE A
SCREEN SAVER

If you do not use your computer for a certain period of time, you can have a screen saver automatically appear. A screen saver is a picture that constantly moves on your screen.

Use a Screen Saver

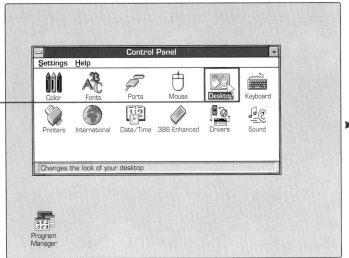

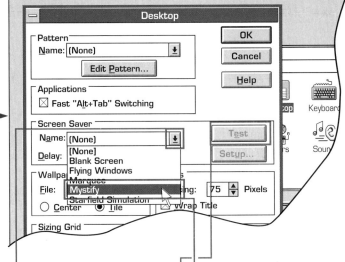

1 To start the **Desktop** program, move the mouse ⬚ over its icon and then quickly press the left button twice.

*Note: To open the **Control Panel**, refer to page 178.*

2 Move the mouse ⬚ over the arrow ⬇ under **Screen Saver** and then press the left button.

◆ A list of the available screen savers appears.

3 Move the mouse ⬚ over the screen saver you want to use (example: **Mystify**) and then press the left button.

◆ To see a demonstration of the screen saver you selected, move the mouse ⬚ over **Test** and then press the left button.

Accessories   Print   **Control
Panel**   Run DOS
in Windows   Sharing
Data   Improve Windows
Performance

Open the Control Panel
Change Date and Time
Change Screen Colors
Add Wallpaper
Use a Screen Saver
Change Mouse Settings
Install Fonts

TIP

◆ Screen savers eliminate "screen burn" which occurs when an image appears in a fixed position for a long period of time. Screen savers are also widely used because of their entertainment value.

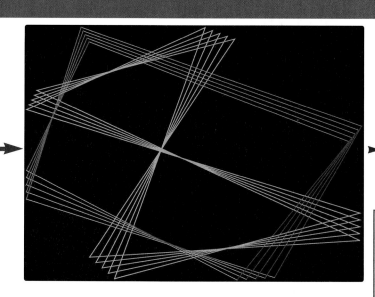

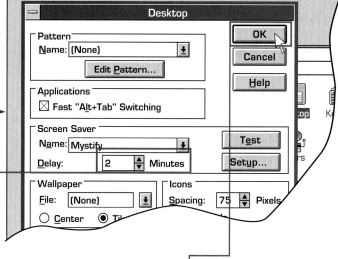

◆ A demonstration of the screen saver appears.

4 Move the mouse on your desk to stop the demonstration.

◆ This box displays the number of minutes of inactivity before the screen saver appears.

5 To change the delay time, move the mouse ⌖ over the box beside **Delay:** and then quickly press the left button twice. Then type a new delay time.

6 To select the screen saver, move the mouse ⌖ over **OK** and then press the left button.

CHANGE MOUSE SETTINGS

You can change the way your mouse works by customizing its speed, appearance and function to suit your needs.

Change Mouse Settings

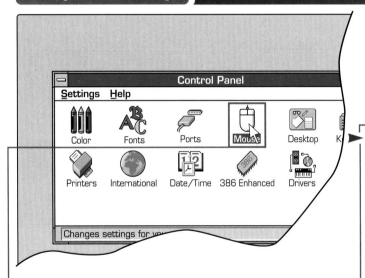

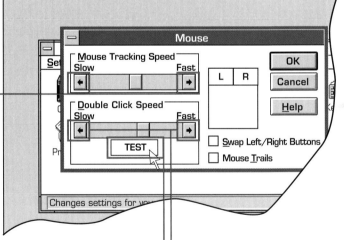

1 To start the **Mouse** program, move the mouse ⤢ over its icon and then quickly press the left button twice.

*Note: To open the **Control Panel**, refer to page 178.*

Change mouse ⤢ speed

2 To change the speed of the mouse ⤢ on your screen, move the mouse ⤢ over the left or right arrow and then press the left button.

*Note: The changes you make in the **Mouse** dialog box take effect immediately.*

Change double click speed

3 To change the speed that Windows registers a double-click, move the mouse ⤢ over the left or right arrow and then press the left button.

4 To test the new double-click speed, move the mouse ⤢ over the **TEST** box and then quickly press the left button twice. **TEST** becomes highlighted if you clicked at the correct speed.

Accessories | Print | **Control Panel** | Run DOS in Windows | Sharing Data | Improve Windows Performance

Open the Control Panel
Change Date and Time
Change Screen Colors
Add Wallpaper
Use a Screen Saver
Change Mouse Settings
Install Fonts

TIPS

◆ The **Mouse** dialog box displayed on your screen may be different than shown below. There are many versions of mouse software available and each one displays a different **Mouse** dialog box.

◆ If you have a portable computer, the Mouse Trails option can improve the visibility of the mouse on your screen.

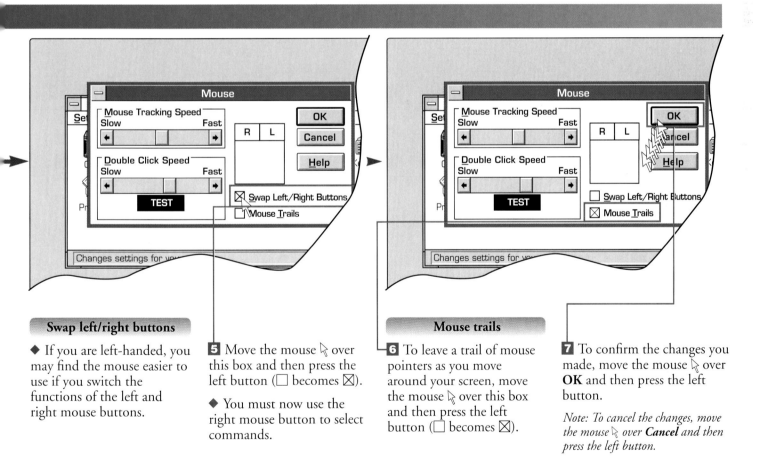

Swap left/right buttons

◆ If you are left-handed, you may find the mouse easier to use if you switch the functions of the left and right mouse buttons.

5 Move the mouse over this box and then press the left button (□ becomes ☒).

◆ You must now use the right mouse button to select commands.

Mouse trails

6 To leave a trail of mouse pointers as you move around your screen, move the mouse over this box and then press the left button (□ becomes ☒).

7 To confirm the changes you made, move the mouse over **OK** and then press the left button.

*Note: To cancel the changes, move the mouse over **Cancel** and then press the left button.*

INSTALL FONTS

Windows offers a limited number of fonts. To provide more variety when creating documents, you can install additional fonts.

What is a Font?

FONT

A font refers to the design of the characters. Some examples are:

Arial

Courier New

Letter Gothic

Times New Roman

TYPE SIZE

You can change the size of each font to make the characters larger or smaller. Some examples are:

5

10

15

20

25

Note: Windows measures size in points. There are approximately 72 points per inch.

TYPE STYLE

You can change the style of each font. Some examples are:

Bold

Italic

<u>Underline</u>

Shadow

Outline

Windows provides you with TrueType fonts. These fonts print exactly the way they display on your screen. This is known as WYSIWYG (What You See Is What You Get).

TrueType fonts are scalable. This means you can produce characters in varying sizes.

You can use different fonts to turn a dull and lifeless letter into an interesting, attractive document.

INSTALL
FONTS

Windows enables you to install additional fonts on your computer. You can then use these fonts to enhance the appearance of your documents.

Install Fonts

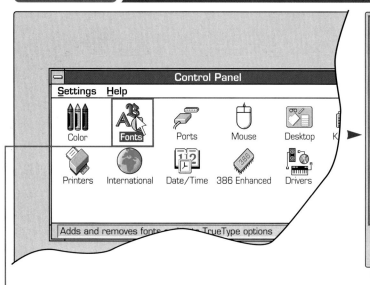

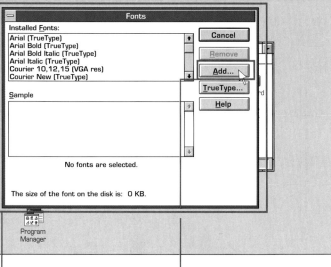

1 To start the **Fonts** program, move the mouse Ⓡ over its icon and then quickly press the left button twice.

*Note: To open the **Control Panel**, refer to page 178.*

◆ The **Fonts** dialog box appears.

2 Move the mouse Ⓡ over **Add** and then press the left button.

Accessories   Print   **Control Panel**   Run DOS in Windows   Sharing Data   Improve Windows Performance

Open the Control Panel
Change Date and Time
Change Screen Colors
Add Wallpaper
Use a Screen Saver
Change Mouse Settings
Install Fonts

TIP

You can purchase fonts stored on diskettes at most computer stores.

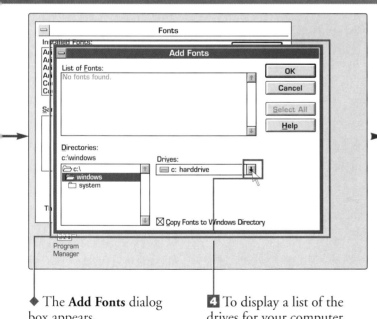

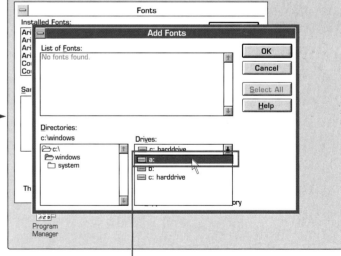

◆ The **Add Fonts** dialog box appears.

3 Insert the diskette containing the fonts you want to install into a drive (example: **a:**).

4 To display a list of the drives for your computer, move the mouse ⌖ over the arrow ⊥ under **Drives:** and then press the left button.

5 To select the drive containing the diskette, move the mouse ⌖ over the drive (example: **a:**) and then press the left button.

◆ Windows retrieves the fonts from the diskette.

Note: To continue the installation, refer to the next page.

INSTALL FONTS

When installing fonts, Windows displays the names of all the fonts on the diskette you supplied. You can install some or all of these fonts.

Install Fonts (Continued)

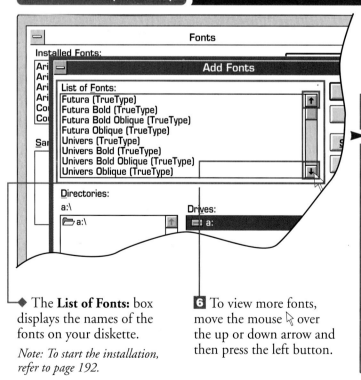

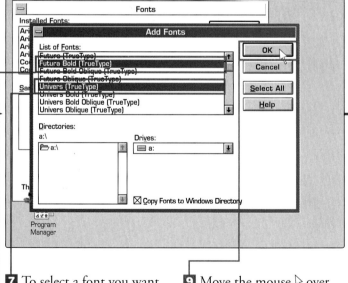

◆ The **List of Fonts:** box displays the names of the fonts on your diskette.

Note: To start the installation, refer to page 192.

6 To view more fonts, move the mouse ⬚ over the up or down arrow and then press the left button.

7 To select a font you want to install, move the mouse ⬚ over the font and then press the left button.

8 To select additional fonts, press and hold down **Ctrl** and then repeat step **7** for each font you want to install.

9 Move the mouse ⬚ over **OK** and then press the left button.

| Accessories | Print | **Control Panel** | Run DOS in Windows | Sharing Data | Improve Windows Performance |

Open the Control Panel
Change Date and Time
Change Screen Colors
Add Wallpaper
Use a Screen Saver
Change Mouse Settings
Install Fonts

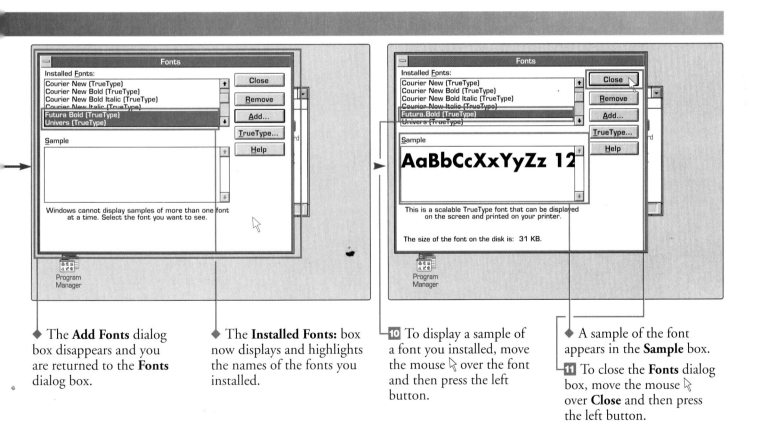

TIP

Select All **You can quickly select and then install all the fonts on your diskette by using the Select All button.**

To select all the fonts, replace steps **7** and **8** on page 194 with the following: Move the mouse ⤷ over **Select All** and then press the left button.

◆ The **Add Fonts** dialog box disappears and you are returned to the **Fonts** dialog box.

◆ The **Installed Fonts:** box now displays and highlights the names of the fonts you installed.

10 To display a sample of a font you installed, move the mouse ⤷ over the font and then press the left button.

◆ A sample of the font appears in the **Sample** box.

11 To close the **Fonts** dialog box, move the mouse ⤷ over **Close** and then press the left button.

DISPLAY THE DOS PROMPT

- Type EXIT and press ENTER to quit this MS–DOS prompt and return to Windows.
- Press ALT+TAB to switch to Windows or another application.
- Press ALT+ENTER to switch this MS–DOS Prompt between a window and full screen.

Microsoft(R) MS–DOS(R) Version 5
     (C)Copyright Microsoft Corp 1981–1993.

C:\WINDOWS>VER

MS–DOS Version 5.00

C:\WINDOWS>_

You can use DOS commands and programs without having to exit Windows.

Display the DOS Prompt

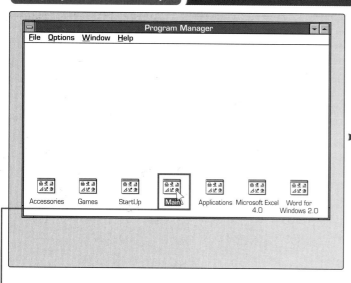

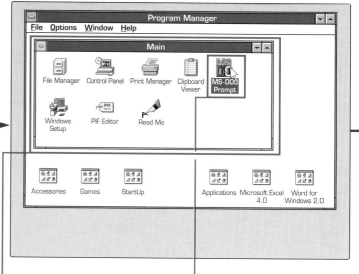

1 To open the **Main** group window, move the mouse over its icon and then quickly press the left button twice.

◆ The **Main** group window opens.

2 To display the MS-DOS prompt, move the mouse over its icon and then quickly press the left button twice.

196

Display the DOS Prompt
Display DOS in a Window
Start a DOS Program
Display DOS Program in a Window
Tile Windows

IMPORTANT

Do not use the following commands when displaying the MS-DOS prompt through Windows:

CHKDSK /F
UNDELETE
CHCP

Furthermore, do not use any disk optimization or defragmentation programs.

To use any of these commands or programs, you must first completely exit Windows.

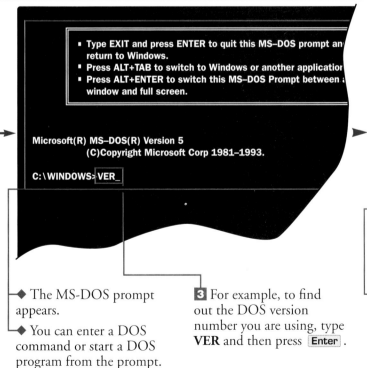

◆ The MS-DOS prompt appears.

◆ You can enter a DOS command or start a DOS program from the prompt.

3 For example, to find out the DOS version number you are using, type **VER** and then press `Enter`.

◆ The DOS version number you are using appears.

DISPLAY DOS IN A WINDOW

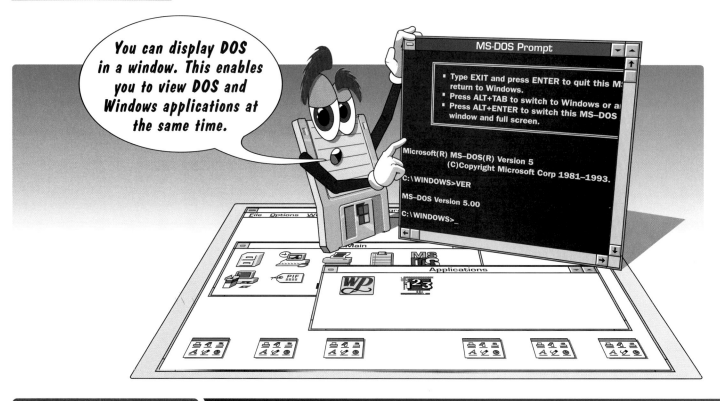

You can display DOS in a window. This enables you to view DOS and Windows applications at the same time.

Display DOS in a Window

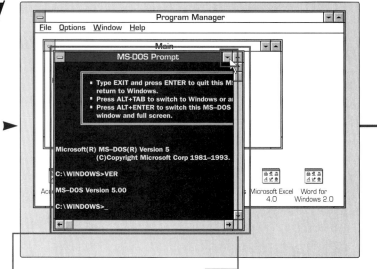

1 To display DOS in a window, press and hold down `Alt` and then press `Enter`.

Note: To display the DOS prompt, refer to page 196.

◆ DOS appears in a window.

◆ You can move and size the window.

Note: To move a window, refer to page 12. To size a window, refer to page 14.

2 To reduce the DOS window to an icon, move the mouse ▷ over its **Minimize** button and then press the left button.

Display the DOS Prompt
Display DOS in a Window
Start a DOS Program
Display DOS Program in a Window
Tile Windows

IMPORTANT

To display DOS in a window, you must have the following:

◆ A 386 (or higher) computer

◆ At least 2 megabytes of electronic memory (RAM)

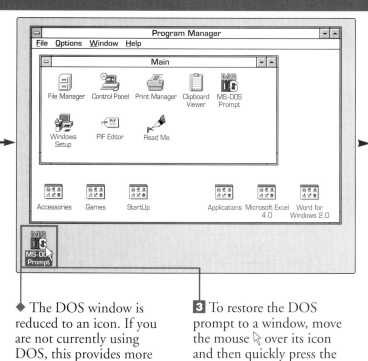

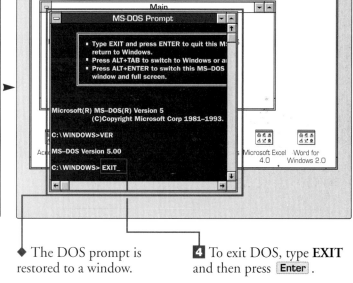

◆ The DOS window is reduced to an icon. If you are not currently using DOS, this provides more working space on your screen.

3 To restore the DOS prompt to a window, move the mouse ⌖ over its icon and then quickly press the left button twice.

◆ The DOS prompt is restored to a window.

4 To exit DOS, type **EXIT** and then press `Enter`.

START A DOS PROGRAM

You can start a DOS program directly from Windows. This enables you to take advantage of some Windows features.

Start a DOS Program

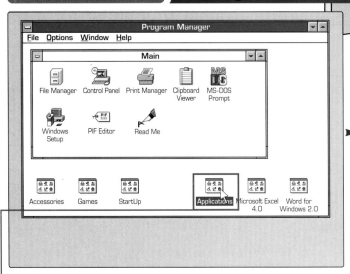

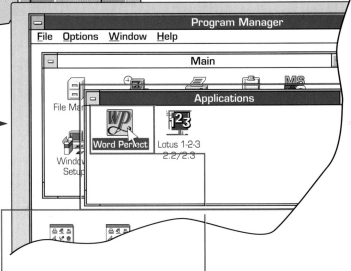

1 To open the **Applications** group window, move the mouse ⇖ over its icon and then quickly press the left button twice.

◆ The **Applications** group window opens.

◆ When you installed Windows, you had the option of creating an icon for each DOS program on your computer. The **Applications** group window contains these icons.

2 To start a program (example: **WordPerfect**), move the mouse ⇖ over its icon and then quickly press the left button twice.

200

Accessories   Print   Control   **Run DOS**   Sharing   Improve Windows
                                     Panel   **in Windows**   Data   Performance

Display the DOS Prompt
Display DOS in a Window
Start a DOS Program
Display DOS Program in a Window
Tile Windows

Doc 1 Pg 1 Ln 1" Pos 1"

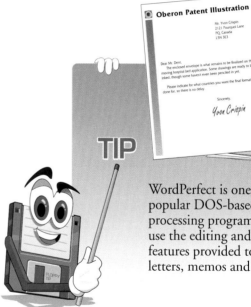

TIP

WordPerfect is one of the most popular DOS-based word processing programs. You can use the editing and formatting features provided to produce letters, memos and reports.

◆ The program starts.

◆ You can use the program as if you were running it in regular DOS. When you exit the program, you are returned to Windows.

DISPLAY DOS PROGRAM IN A WINDOW

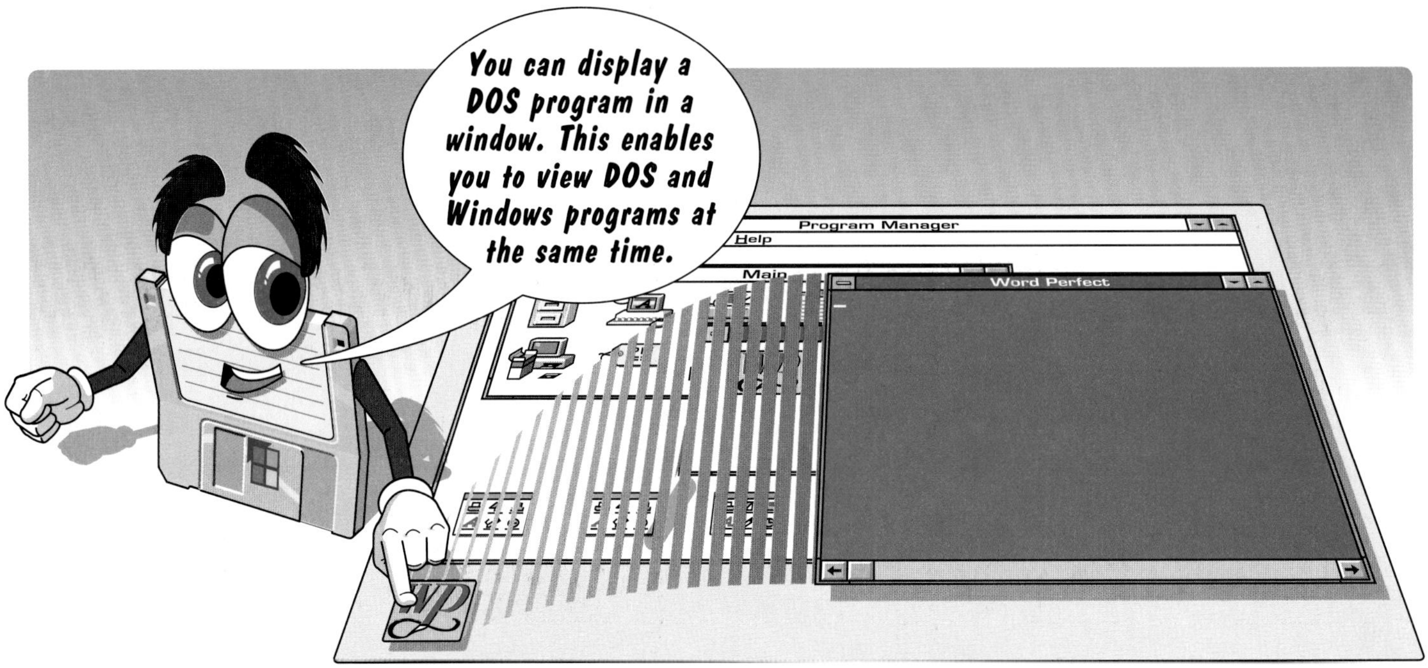

You can display a DOS program in a window. This enables you to view DOS and Windows programs at the same time.
Program Manager
Help
Main
Word Perfect

Display DOS Program in a Window

Doc 1 Pg 1 Ln 1" Pos 1"

1 To display a DOS program in a window, press and hold down Alt and then press Enter.

Note: To start a DOS program, refer to page 200.

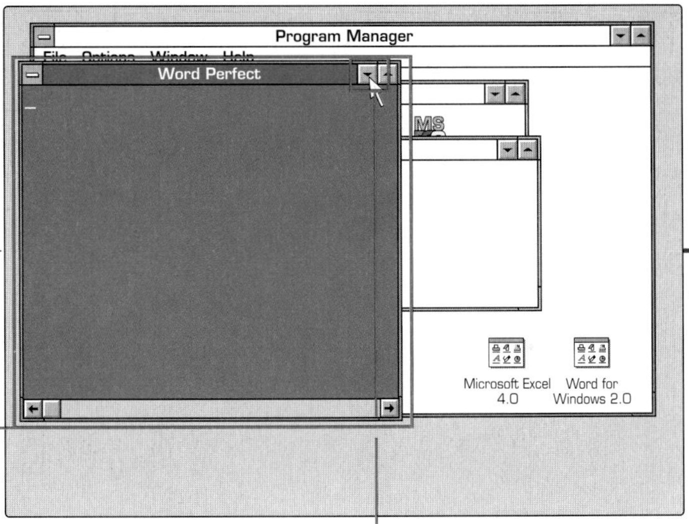

Program Manager
Word Perfect
Microsoft Excel 4.0
Word for Windows 2.0

◆ The DOS program appears in a window.

◆ You can move and size the window.

Note: To move a window, refer to page 12. To size a window, refer to page 14.

2 To reduce the DOS window to an icon, move the mouse over its **Minimize** button and then press the left button.

Display the DOS Prompt
Display DOS in a Window
Start a DOS Program
Display DOS Program in a Window
Tile Windows

IMPORTANT

To display a DOS program in a window, you must have the following:

◆ A 386 (or higher) computer

◆ At least 2 megabytes of electronic memory (RAM)

SWITCH BETWEEN APPLICATIONS

Program Manager

1 To quickly switch between applications, press and hold down Alt .

2 Still holding down Alt , press Tab until the name of the application you want to switch to appears.

3 Release Alt and the application becomes active.

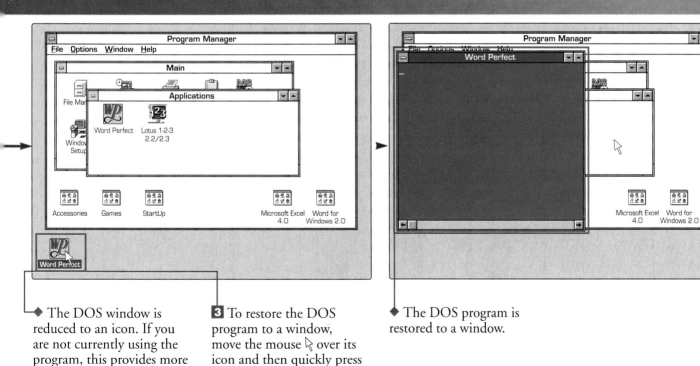

◆ The DOS window is reduced to an icon. If you are not currently using the program, this provides more working space on your screen.

3 To restore the DOS program to a window, move the mouse ⍺ over its icon and then quickly press the left button twice.

◆ The DOS program is restored to a window.

TILE
WINDOWS

If you have several DOS and Windows programs open on your screen, some of them may be hidden from view. You can use the Tile command to place all the open windows side-by-side without overlapping them.

Tile Windows

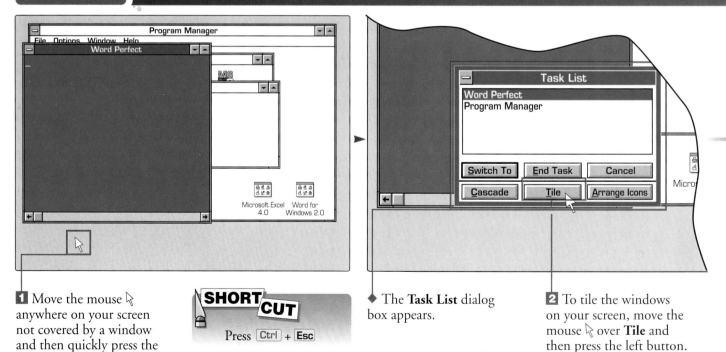

1 Move the mouse ⬁ anywhere on your screen not covered by a window and then quickly press the left button twice.

SHORT CUT

Press Ctrl + Esc

◆ The **Task List** dialog box appears.

2 To tile the windows on your screen, move the mouse ⬁ over **Tile** and then press the left button.

| Accessories | Print | Control Panel | **Run DOS in Windows** | Sharing Data | Improve Windows Performance |

Display the DOS Prompt
Display DOS in a Window
Start a DOS Program
Display DOS Program in a Window
Tile Windows

EXIT WORDPERFECT

1 To make the **WordPerfect** window active, move the mouse ⬉ anywhere over its window and then press the left button.

2 Press **F7**.

3 To exit WordPerfect without saving the document, press **N** (for **No**).

4 To exit WordPerfect, press **Y** (for **Yes**).

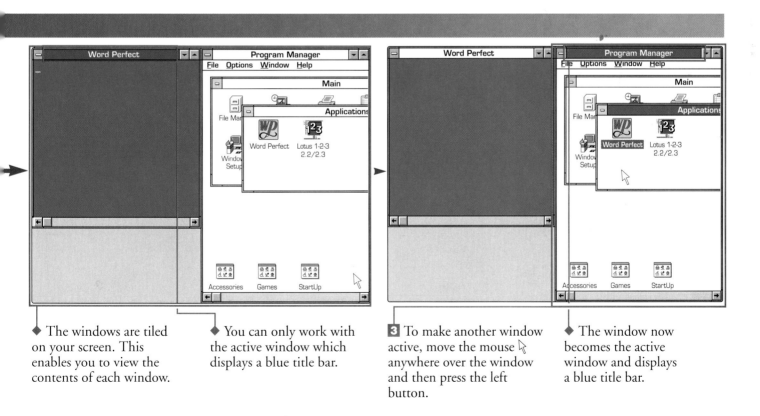

◆ The windows are tiled on your screen. This enables you to view the contents of each window.

◆ You can only work with the active window which displays a blue title bar.

3 To make another window active, move the mouse ⬉ anywhere over the window and then press the left button.

◆ The window now becomes the active window and displays a blue title bar.

> *You can share data between applications in Windows. There are three ways to share data: Copying, Linking and Embedding.*

Copying

◆ You can copy data from one application and place it in another. Both applications will then display the data.

◆ Use the copy method when you do not want to change the data shared between applications.

To change the data, you must repeat the copy procedure.

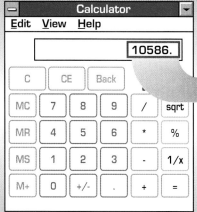

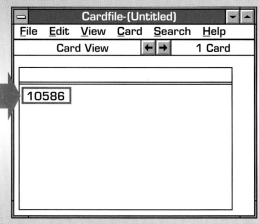

Terms You Need to Know to Link or Embed an Object

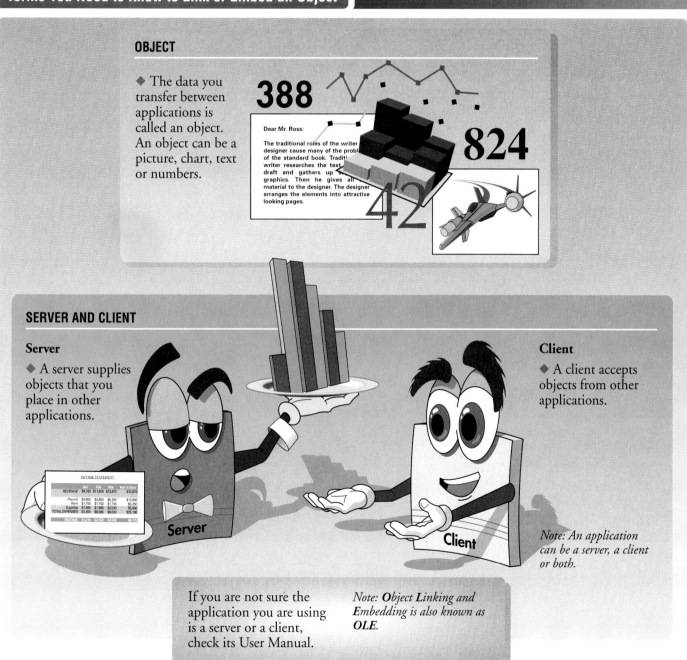

OBJECT

◆ The data you transfer between applications is called an object. An object can be a picture, chart, text or numbers.

SERVER AND CLIENT

Server

◆ A server supplies objects that you place in other applications.

Client

◆ A client accepts objects from other applications.

Note: An application can be a server, a client or both.

If you are not sure the application you are using is a server or a client, check its User Manual.

*Note: **Object Linking and Embedding** is also known as **OLE**.*

Linking

Q: Do I have to save an object I want to link to a client document?

A: Yes! You must save an object in the server application before you can link it to a client document.

Q: When should I link an object?

A: Link an object when you want changes to the server object to automatically appear in all linked client documents.

Q: What command do I use?

A: To link an object, use the **Paste Link** command.

Q: How do I edit a linked object?

A: Double clicking the object in the client document opens the server application that supplied the object.

◆ Any changes you make to the object in the server application automatically appear in all linked client documents.

When you link an object, the client document receives a "screen image" of the object. The real object resides in the server document.

Paintbrush - LOGO.BMP

File   Edit   View   Text   Pick   Options   Help

SERVER DOCUMENT

Write - ONE.WRI
File   Edit   Find
Character   Paragraph
Document   Help

Page 1
CLIENT DOCUMENT
containing linked object

Write - TWO.W
File   Edit   Find
Character   Para
Document   Help

Page 1
CLIENT DOCUMENT
containing linked object

Embedding

Q: Do I have to save an object I want to embed in a client document?

A: No! You do not have to save an object in the server application before embedding it in a client document.

Q: When should I embed an object?

A: Embed an object when you want it to become part of the client document. This makes the document more portable since the server document is not required.

Q: What command do I use?

A: To embed an object, use the **Paste** command.

*Note: If the applications you are using support OLE, using the **Paste** command embeds the object. If the applications do not support OLE, using the **Paste** command copies the object.*

Q: How do I edit an embedded object?

A: Double clicking the object in the client document opens the server application that supplied the object.

◆ Any changes you make to the object only appear in the client document containing the object.

Note: After you embed an object in the client document, the server document is no longer required.

◆ Documents containing embedded objects require more memory than documents linked to objects.

COPY
DATA

You can copy data from one document and place it in another. Both documents will then display the data.

Copy Data Between Applications

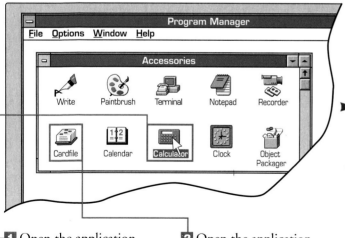

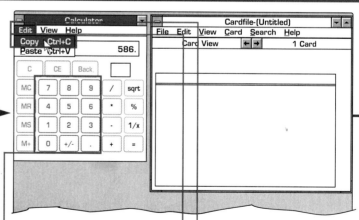

1 Open the application you want to copy data **from**.

To open **Calculator**, move the mouse ⟍ over its icon and then quickly press the left button twice.

2 Open the application you want to copy data **to**.

To open **Cardfile**, move the mouse ⟍ over its icon and then quickly press the left button twice.

3 To enter numbers into the calculator, move the mouse ⟍ over the numbers and then press the left button (example: 5, 8, 6).

*Note: To minimize the **Program Manager** window, refer to page 20. To tile the windows on your screen, refer to page 41.*

4 To copy the data, move the mouse ⟍ over **Edit** and then press the left button.

5 Move the mouse ⟍ over **Copy** and then press the left button.

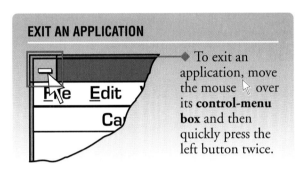

EXIT AN APPLICATION

◆ To exit an application, move the mouse ⬚ over its **control-menu box** and then quickly press the left button twice.

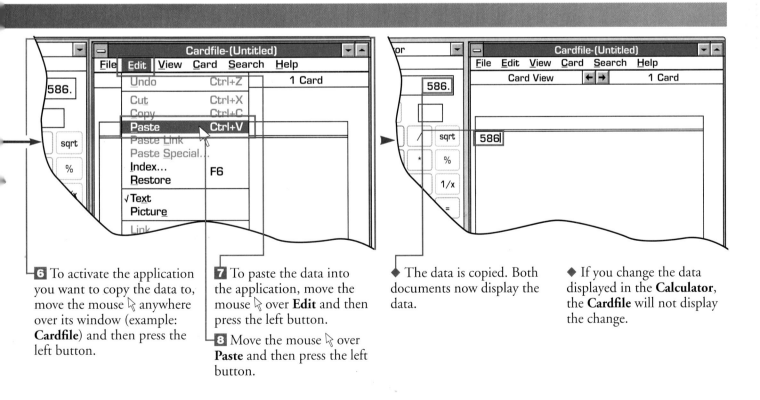

6 To activate the application you want to copy the data to, move the mouse ⬚ anywhere over its window (example: **Cardfile**) and then press the left button.

7 To paste the data into the application, move the mouse ⬚ over **Edit** and then press the left button.

8 Move the mouse ⬚ over **Paste** and then press the left button.

◆ The data is copied. Both documents now display the data.

◆ If you change the data displayed in the **Calculator**, the **Cardfile** will not display the change.

CREATE
AN OBJECT

> The data you transfer between documents is called an object. An object can be a picture, chart, text or numbers.

Object

Server

Client

Create an Object

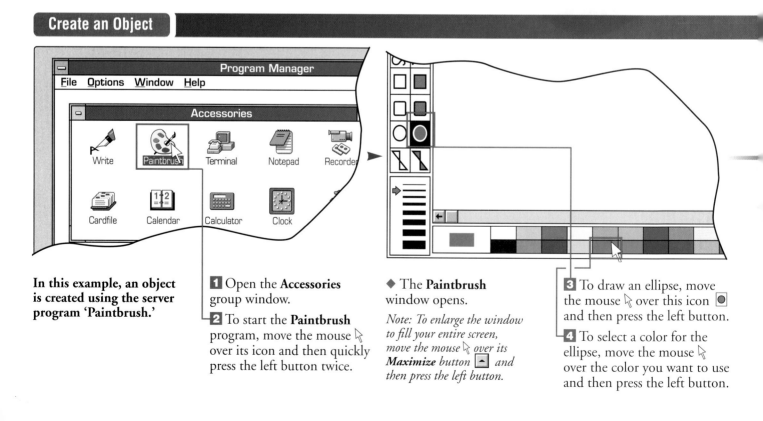

In this example, an object is created using the server program 'Paintbrush.'

1 Open the **Accessories** group window.

2 To start the **Paintbrush** program, move the mouse ⬡ over its icon and then quickly press the left button twice.

◆ The **Paintbrush** window opens.

*Note: To enlarge the window to fill your entire screen, move the mouse ⬡ over its **Maximize** button ▲ and then press the left button.*

3 To draw an ellipse, move the mouse ⬡ over this icon ⬤ and then press the left button.

4 To select a color for the ellipse, move the mouse ⬡ over the color you want to use and then press the left button.

212

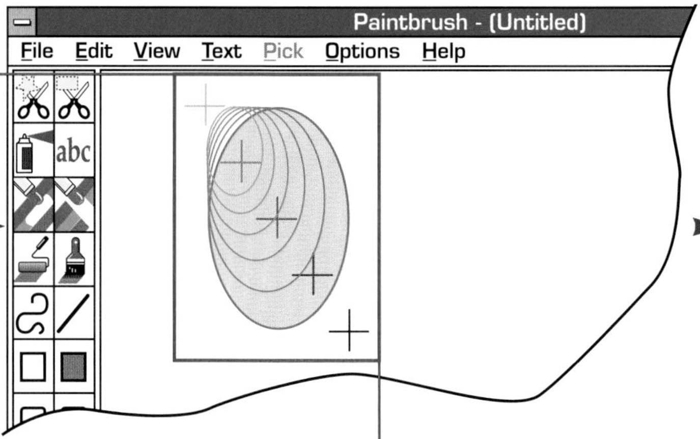

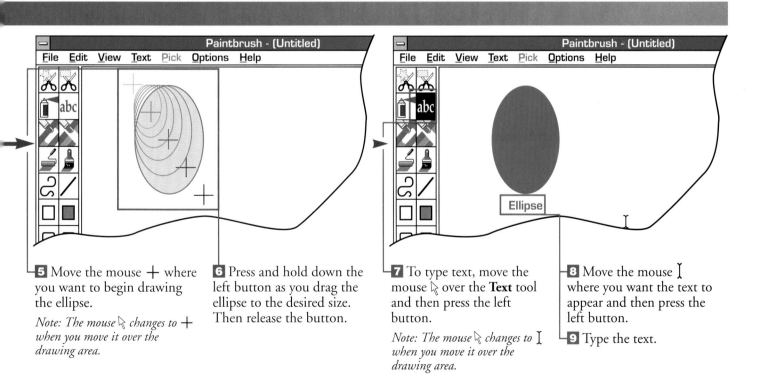

5 Move the mouse + where you want to begin drawing the ellipse.

Note: The mouse ↖ changes to + when you move it over the drawing area.

6 Press and hold down the left button as you drag the ellipse to the desired size. Then release the button.

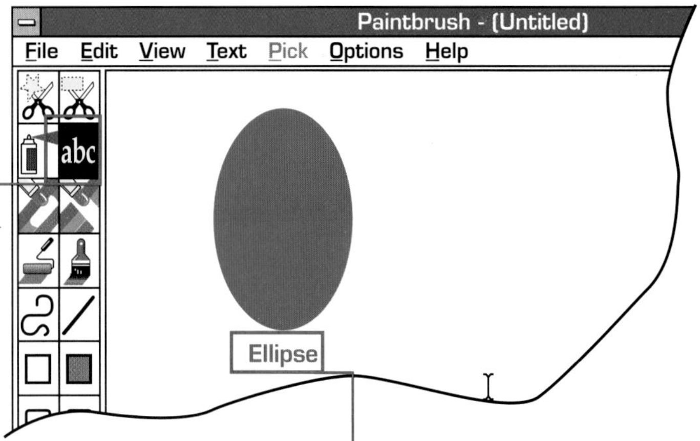

7 To type text, move the mouse ↖ over the **Text** tool and then press the left button.

Note: The mouse ↖ changes to I when you move it over the drawing area.

8 Move the mouse I where you want the text to appear and then press the left button.

9 Type the text.

SAVE
AN OBJECT

You must save an object you created before linking it to a client document. Saving a document stores it in your computer.

Save an Object

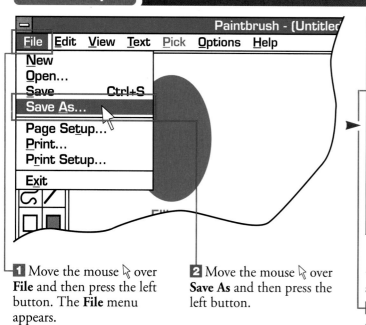

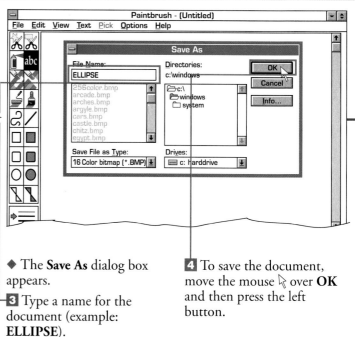

1 Move the mouse ▷ over **File** and then press the left button. The **File** menu appears.

2 Move the mouse ▷ over **Save As** and then press the left button.

◆ The **Save As** dialog box appears.

3 Type a name for the document (example: **ELLIPSE**).

4 To save the document, move the mouse ▷ over **OK** and then press the left button.

Accessories   Print   Control   Run DOS   **Sharing**   Improve Windows
                                     Panel   in Windows   **Data**   Performance

Introduction   Link an Object
Copy Data   Edit a Linked Object
Create an Object   Edit an Embedded Object
Save an Object

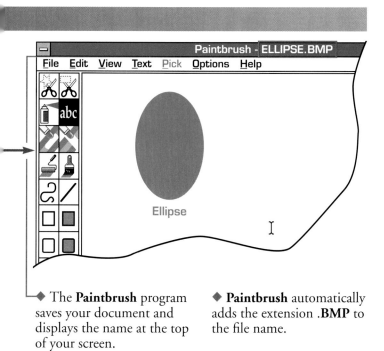

EMBED AN OBJECT

You do not have to save an object you want to embed in a client document.

◆ The **Paintbrush** program saves your document and displays the name at the top of your screen.

◆ **Paintbrush** automatically adds the extension **.BMP** to the file name.

LINK
AN OBJECT

After you create and save an object, you can link it to a client document. Both documents will then display the object.

Link an Object

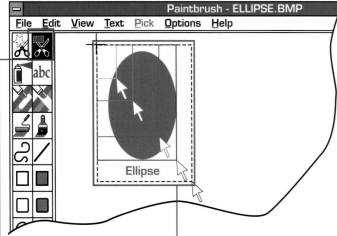

Ellipse

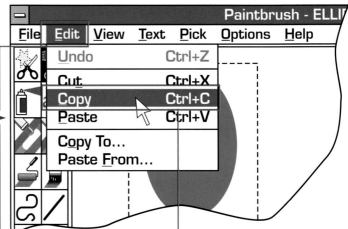

Edit	
Undo	Ctrl+Z
Cut	Ctrl+X
Copy	Ctrl+C
Paste	Ctrl+V
Copy To...	
Paste From...	

1 To select the object in **Paintbrush**, move the mouse ↘ over the **Pick** tool and then press the left button.

Note: The mouse ↘ changes to + when you move it over the drawing area.

2 Move the mouse + over the top left corner of the object.

3 Press and hold down the left button as you drag the mouse ↘ until a box surrounds the object. Then release the button.

4 Move the mouse ↘ over **Edit** and then press the left button. The **Edit** menu appears.

5 Move the mouse ↘ over **Copy** and then press the left button.

◆ Your computer stores a copy of the object in its electronic memory.

In the example below, an object created in Paintbrush is linked to a document in Write.

Write receives a "screen image" of the object. The real object still resides in Paintbrush.

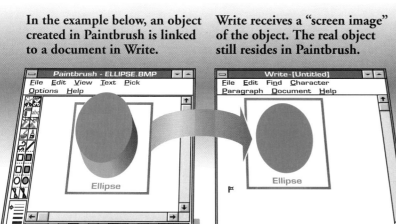

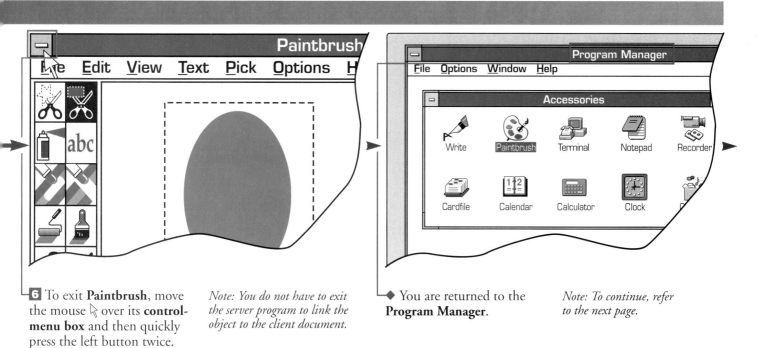

6 To exit **Paintbrush**, move the mouse ⤹ over its **control-menu box** and then quickly press the left button twice.

Note: You do not have to exit the server program to link the object to the client document.

◆ You are returned to the **Program Manager**.

Note: To continue, refer to the next page.

LINK
AN OBJECT

> *To link an object to a client document, you must use the Paste Link command.*

Link an Object (continued)

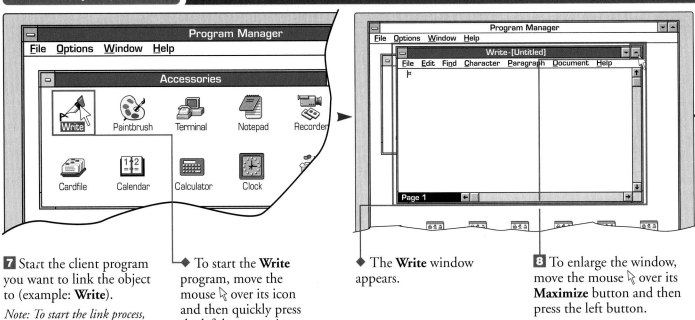

7 Start the client program you want to link the object to (example: **Write**).

Note: To start the link process, refer to page 216.

◆ To start the **Write** program, move the mouse ⌖ over its icon and then quickly press the left button twice.

◆ The **Write** window appears.

8 To enlarge the window, move the mouse ⌖ over its **Maximize** button and then press the left button.

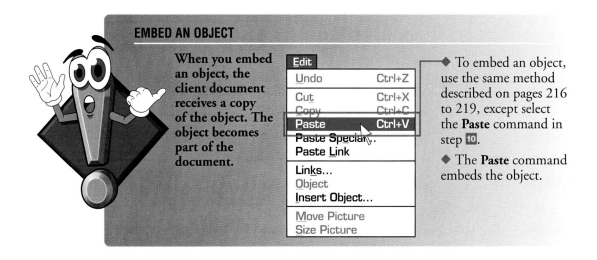

EMBED AN OBJECT

When you embed an object, the client document receives a copy of the object. The object becomes part of the document.

◆ To embed an object, use the same method described on pages 216 to 219, except select the **Paste** command in step **10**.

◆ The **Paste** command embeds the object.

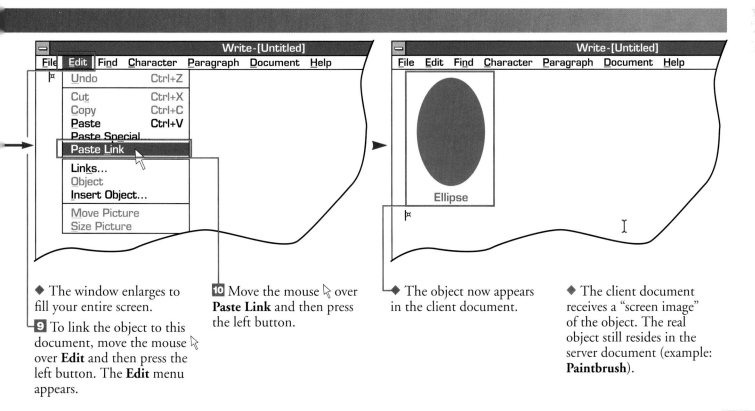

◆ The window enlarges to fill your entire screen.

9 To link the object to this document, move the mouse ⟍ over **Edit** and then press the left button. The **Edit** menu appears.

10 Move the mouse ⟍ over **Paste Link** and then press the left button.

◆ The object now appears in the client document.

◆ The client document receives a "screen image" of the object. The real object still resides in the server document (example: **Paintbrush**).

EDIT A LINKED OBJECT

You can easily make changes to a linked object. If you save these changes, they will appear in all client documents linked to the object.

Edit a Linked Object

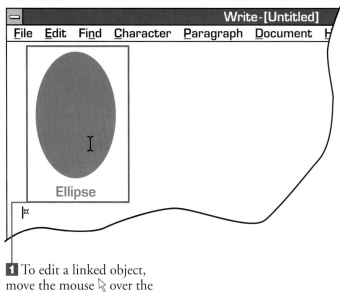

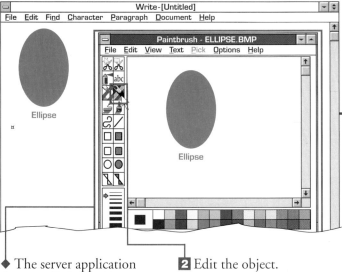

1 To edit a linked object, move the mouse ⇱ over the object and then quickly press the left button twice.

◆ The server application that supplied the object opens (example: **Paintbrush**).

Note: To move a window, refer to page 12. To size a window, refer to page 14.

2 Edit the object.

For example, to use the eraser, move the mouse ⇱ over the **Eraser** tool and then press the left button.

SAVE CHANGES

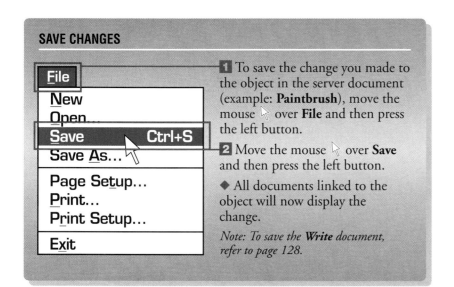

1 To save the change you made to the object in the server document (example: **Paintbrush**), move the mouse over **File** and then press the left button.

2 Move the mouse over **Save** and then press the left button.

◆ All documents linked to the object will now display the change.

*Note: To save the **Write** document, refer to page 128.*

EXIT AN APPLICATION

◆ To exit an application, move the mouse over its **control-menu box** and then quickly press the left button twice.

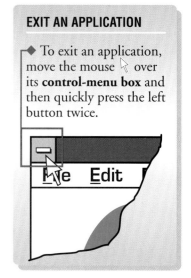

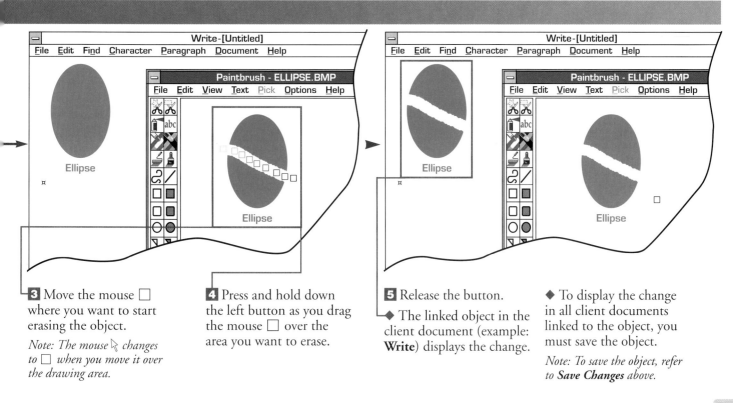

3 Move the mouse □ where you want to start erasing the object.

Note: The mouse changes to □ when you move it over the drawing area.

4 Press and hold down the left button as you drag the mouse □ over the area you want to erase.

5 Release the button.

◆ The linked object in the client document (example: **Write**) displays the change.

◆ To display the change in all client documents linked to the object, you must save the object.

*Note: To save the object, refer to **Save Changes** above.*

EDIT AN EMBEDDED OBJECT

You can easily make changes to an embedded object. These changes will only appear in the document containing the object.

Edit an Embedded Object

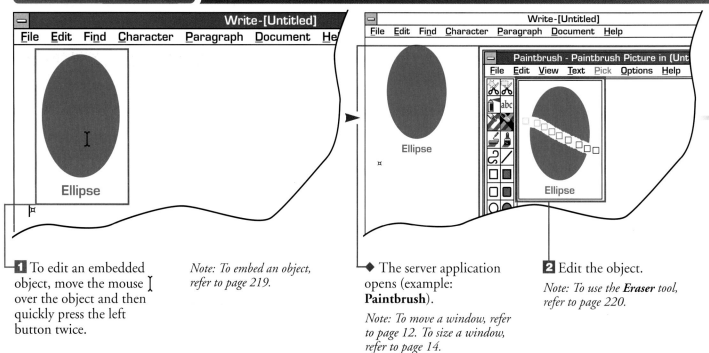

1 To edit an embedded object, move the mouse ⌶ over the object and then quickly press the left button twice.

Note: To embed an object, refer to page 219.

◆ The server application opens (example: **Paintbrush**).

Note: To move a window, refer to page 12. To size a window, refer to page 14.

2 Edit the object.

*Note: To use the **Eraser** tool, refer to page 220.*

Introduction   Link an Object
Copy Data   Edit a Linked Object
Create an Object   **Edit an Embedded Object**
Save an Object

EXIT AN APPLICATION

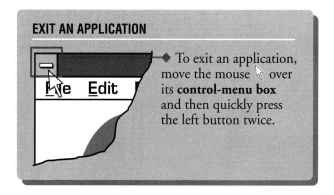

◆ To exit an application, move the mouse ₖ over its **control-menu box** and then quickly press the left button twice.

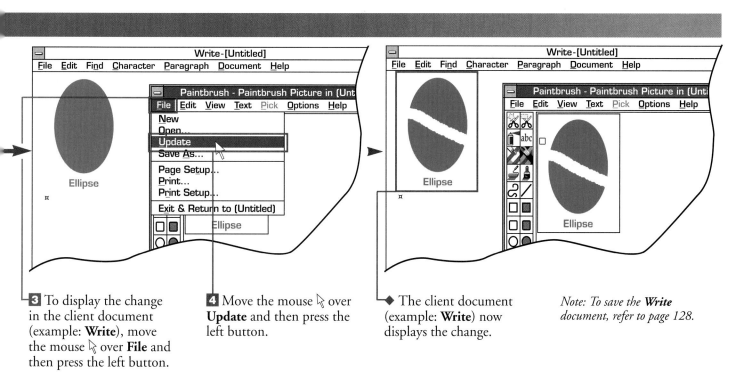

3 To display the change in the client document (example: **Write**), move the mouse ₖ over **File** and then press the left button.

4 Move the mouse ₖ over **Update** and then press the left button.

◆ The client document (example: **Write**) now displays the change.

*Note: To save the **Write** document, refer to page 128.*

You can improve Windows performance by optimizing your computer's hardware and software.

INCREASE ELECTRONIC MEMORY

Electronic memory (RAM) temporarily stores information in your computer. You can avoid "Out of memory" messages and slow computer operation by ensuring your computer has enough RAM.

CPU UPGRADE

The Central Processing Unit (CPU) is the "brain" of your computer. You can upgrade the CPU to increase your computer's performance by as much as 70%.

HARD DRIVE TUNE-UP

A hard drive stores your programs and data. You can improve hard drive performance by using the Check Disk command, Defragmenter and DoubleSpace programs.

VIDEO ADAPTER UPGRADE

You can upgrade your video adapter to speed up the time it takes for images to appear on your monitor.

Electronic memory temporarily stores information inside your computer. It is also known as Random Access Memory or RAM.

You can add more electronic memory to your computer. This enables you to:

◆ make applications run faster

◆ work with larger documents and spreadsheets

◆ work with more applications at the same time

Electronic memory and your desk have similar properties. The larger your desk, the more documents you can display at once.

Similarly, the more electronic memory in your computer, the more applications you can work with at the same time.

WORKING WITH WINDOWS

Accessories   Print   Control   Run DOS   Sharing   **Improve Windows**
                                    Panel   in Windows   Data   **Performance**

Introduction
Electronic Memory
Central Processing Unit
Video Adapter
Hard Drive

Windows Operating Modes

**Windows operates in either the
Standard or 386 Enhanced Mode:**

STANDARD MODE
(FOR 286 COMPUTERS)

If you have a 286
computer, Windows will
operate in the standard
mode.

An "Out of memory" message appears if your
computer runs out of electronic memory. You
must add more memory to your computer or free
up memory by closing some applications.

386 ENHANCED MODE (FOR 386
OR HIGHER COMPUTERS)

If you have a 386
or higher computer,
Windows will operate
in the enhanced mode.

A computer running in this mode can "substitute"
hard drive space for electronic memory (RAM). This
memory is known as "virtual" memory and is much
slower than RAM.

If your computer becomes sluggish after starting
an application and your hard drive light comes on
when you choose a command, your computer is
using virtual memory. To improve performance,
add more electronic memory to your computer or
close some applications.

TIP To improve Windows
performance, increase
the electronic memory
in your computer from
4MB to 8MB. This can
make applications run
faster.

CENTRAL PROCESSING UNIT

VIDEO ADAPTER

The Central Processing Unit (CPU) is the "brain" of your computer. To improve Windows performance, you can purchase an OverDrive CPU.

Note: The CPU is also known as the microprocessor.

OverDrive CPU

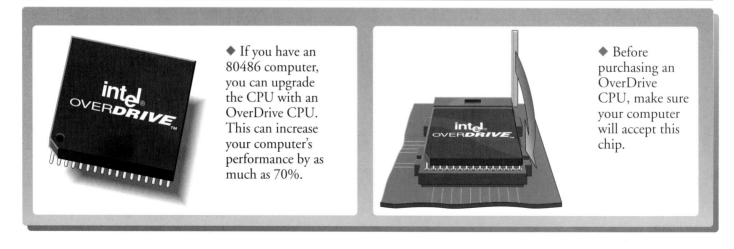

◆ If you have an 80486 computer, you can upgrade the CPU with an OverDrive CPU. This can increase your computer's performance by as much as 70%.

◆ Before purchasing an OverDrive CPU, make sure your computer will accept this chip.

A video adapter generates the images that appear on your monitor. The faster the video adapter works, the faster the images will appear.

◆ **Monitor**

The monitor displays the information sent from the video adapter.

◆ A cable connects the video adapter to your monitor.

◆ **Video Adapter Card**

Types of Video Adapters

FRAME BUFFER

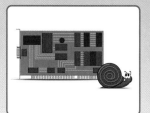

◆ Slow
◆ Inexpensive

A frame buffer video adapter takes more time to generate the images appearing on your monitor.

ACCELERATOR

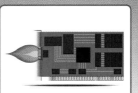

◆ Fast
◆ More expensive

You can install an accelerated video adapter to speed up the time it takes for images to appear on your monitor.

TIP The resolution and number of colors displayed on your screen affect the speed of a video adapter. To improve Windows performance, set your screen display at the lowest resolution, with the least number of colors that you find acceptable.

Consult your user manual for details on changing your screen setup.

HARD
DRIVE

A hard drive stores your programs and data on a stack of rotating disks.

You can increase your hard drive performance by using the Check Disk command, Defragmenter and DoubleSpace programs.

Choosing a Hard Drive

You can purchase a larger hard drive to store more programs and data. Select a drive that is much larger than you think you will need. New applications and data inevitably require more storage space.

If you are not sure what hard drive capacity you need, follow these guidelines:

Application	Recommended Capacity
Home	100 – 250MB
Business	250 – 600MB
Power User	600MB Plus

Check Disk

Check Disk
REPORT

62830592 bytes total disk space
79872 bytes in 2 hidden files
26624 bytes in 7 directories
16269312 bytes in 487 user files
46454784 bytes available on disk

2048 bytes in each allocation unit
30679 total allocation units on disk
22683 available allocation units on disk

655360 total bytes memory
636352 bytes free

MS-DOS includes the Check Disk command. You should use this command at least once a week to find and correct problems on your hard drive. Consult your MS-DOS user manual for further information.

Defragmenter

Adding and updating files on your hard drive (especially when its almost full) can break files into pieces and scatter them around the drive. MS-DOS version 6.0 and higher includes a defragmenter program that analyzes the data on the drive and brings all the pieces of each file together.

Use the Defragmenter program twice a month to speed up the time required to retrieve files from your hard drive. Consult your MS-DOS manual for further information.

DoubleSpace

MS-DOS version 6.0 and higher includes a program called DoubleSpace that compresses the information stored on your hard drive. A compressed hard drive will have 50 to 100 percent more free space. Consult your MS-DOS manual for further information.

INDEX